GLOBE

The best of
ROME
AND THE VATICAN

FIONA NICHOLS

NEW
HOLLAND

GLOBETROTTER™

First edition published in 2008
by New Holland Publishers (UK) Ltd
London • Cape Town • Sydney • Auckland
10 9 8 7 6 5 4 3 2 1

website: www.newhollandpublishers.com

Garfield House, 86 Edgware Road
London W2 2EA
United Kingdom

80 McKenzie Street
Cape Town 8001
South Africa

Unit 1, 66 Gibbes Street
Chatswood, NSW 2067
Australia

218 Lake Road
Northcote, Auckland
New Zealand

Distributed in the USA by
The Globe Pequot Press, Connecticut

ISBN 978 1 84773 014 5

Publishing Manager: Thea Grobbelaar
DTP Cartographic Manager: Genené Hart
Editor: Carla Zietsman
Designer: Nicole Bannister
Cartographer: Carryck Wise
Picture Researcher: Zainoenisa Manuel
Consultant: Tracey Gambarotta
Proofreader: Thea Grobbelaar

Reproduction by Resolution (Cape Town)
Printed and bound by Times Offset (M) Sdn. Bhd.,
Malaysia.

This guidebook has been written by independent authors and updaters. The information
therein represents their impartial opinion, and
neither they nor the publishers accept payment
in return for including in the book or writing
more favourable reviews of any of the establishments. Whilst every effort has been made to
ensure that this guidebook is as accurate and up
to date as possible, please be aware that the
facts quoted are subject to change, particularly
the price of food, transport and accommodation. The Publisher accepts no responsibility or
liability for any loss, injury or inconvenience
incurred by readers or travellers using this guide.

Photographic Credits:
Botanica/Photo Access: page 48;
Cubo Images/Photo Access: pages 45, 70, 76;
Nicole Elliott: page 74; **Dario Gaúcho:** page 41;
Fiona Nichols: title page, pages 6–20, 21–24, 27,
28–30, 31–40, 42, 46, 47, 49, 50, 52, 53, 60, 62,
65, 71, 73, 78, 79, 80;
Pictures Colour Library: cover, page 43;
Neil Setchfield: pages 44, 61, 66, 82, 84;
Sime/Photo Access: pages 26, 72, 81, 83;
Jeroen Snijders: page 54

Front Cover: *The Vatican & Ponte St Angelo
over the River Tiber.*
Title Page: *One of Rome's most appealing
flower stalls, in Piazza di Spagna.*

CONTENTS

MAKE THE MOST OF YOUR GUIDE

Reading these two pages will help you to get the most out of your guide and save you time when using it. Sites discussed in the text are cross-referenced with the cover maps – for example, the reference 'Map D–C3' refers to the Rome City Centre Map (Map D), column C, row 3. Use the Map Plan below to quickly locate the map you need.

MAP PLAN

Outside Back Cover   Outside Front Cover

Inside Front Cover   Inside Back Cover

THE BIGGER PICTURE

Key to Map Plan

A – Vatican City
B – St Peter's Basilica
C – Colosseum and
    Surrounds
D – Rome City
    Centre
E – Excursions
F – Hadrian's Villa
G – Trastevere
H – Leonardo da
    Vinci Airport
I – Metro Map

Key to Symbols

✉ — address

☎ — telephone

🖷 — fax

🖳 — website

🖱 — e-mail address

🕓 — opening times

🚌 — tour

💰 — entry fee

🍽 — restaurants nearby

M — nearest metro station

♿ — disabled access

Map Legend

motorway		main road	Via Cavour
national road		other road	Via Sforza
main road		pedestrian mall	VIA CONDOTTI
minor road		city walls	
railway		built-up area	
lake		building of interest	Pantheon
river	Fiume Tevere	museum	Museo Naz. Romano
route numbers	N118 215	college	Collegio Romano
city	ROME	university	Università Gregoriana
major town	⊙ Tivoli	market	Via Sannio Market
town	O Velletri	metro station	M Repubblica
large village	◎ Fiumicino	parking area	P
village	o Nemi	place of worship	△ Sistine Chapel
peaks in metres	M. Cavo 948 m ▲	library	
airport	✈	post office	✉
ruins	Hadrian's Villa	tourist information	i
place of interest	★ Catacombs	one-way street	→
gate	••	police station	●
hotel	Ⓗ LE GRAND	hospital	⊕
park & garden	Orto Botanico		

Keep us Current

Travel information is apt to change, which is why we regularly update our guides. We'd be most grateful to receive feedback from you if you've noted something we should include in our updates. If you have any new information, please share it with us by writing to the Publishing Manager, Globetrotter, at the office nearest to you (addresses on the imprint page of this guide). The most significant contribution to each new edition will be rewarded with a free copy of the updated guide.

Above: *Piazza della Trinità affords fine views over Rome.*

The Hills of Rome
Often quoted in literature, the seven hills of Rome are: **Avertine**, **Capitoline**, **Celian** (or Coelian), **Esquiline**, **Palatine**, **Quirinale** and the **Viminale**.

Climate
Rome enjoys a Mediterranean climate. Its summers are hot and dry but night temperatures are a little lower. Autumn weather in October is glorious with warm days and cool nights. The winter months can also be pleasant, but November sees the most rainfall. April is spring, and it is warm enough to eat out at midday. May can be a marvellous time to visit. Days are warm and rainfall is slightly less than in April.

ROME

If there was ever a city that earned its epithet, it is Rome. The Eternal City has witnessed and shaped 3000 years of history and, remarkably, is still going strong. Thanks to the Great Jubilee celebrations in 2000, many of the buildings were renovated, polished and cleaned. Classical Rome, Medieval Rome and Baroque Rome all received attention as the pollution and decay of decades, even centuries, was carefully buffed away. The Italian capital is, today, simply one of the best-preserved and most beautiful historic cities in the world.

And, within its ancient city confines lies one of the world's smallest independent states, La Città del Vaticano, the Vatican City, home of the Catholic Church and the Pope. It is the final destination for millions of pilgrims intent on visiting the world's largest basilica and, if luck permits, glimpsing their spiritual leader.

The Land

Consisting of just over 300,000km² (115,800 sq miles) of boot-shaped land, Italy has an impressive variety of topographical features and climates. Although the capital was built on seven 'hills', they are really little more than hillocks and Rome is essentially a flat city on a flat, alluvial plain.

The Tiber

Il Tevere, as the Tiber is known in Italian, snakes through Rome, from north to south, separating the western suburbs, the Vatican and Trastevere from the remains of Ancient Rome and the suburbs that run from north, through east and south of the city.

History in Brief

Rome's importance in world history is due to its unique position as the centre of the **Roman Empire** and of **Western Christianity**. The Roman Empire and the papacy have fashioned not just the fabric of Rome, but the geography and civilization of most of Europe. In the case of the Catholic Church, its influence has shaped societies throughout the world.

The Founding of Rome

According to tradition, the history of Rome starts with the twins, **Romulus** and **Remus** (*see* panel, this page), and the founding of Rome in 753BC. After the time of Romulus, Rome was ruled by a succession of seven kings until **Tarquinius Superbus** was driven out in 509BC.

The Republic

Rome subsequently became a republic. Besides the fact that the Romans gradually began enlarging their stronghold, they also exercised influence outside their own geographical area and, by the 3rd century BC, most of Italy fell under Rome's command. Then, the Republic extended so relentlessly that it soon comprised all the territory from Spain to Syria, and from southern France to the north of Africa. In 49BC, the military commander, **Gaius Julius Caesar**, seized power and unconstitutionally declared himself Emperor. He was, however, assassinated in Rome a month later.

Romulus and Remus
The oft-quoted story relates how, in the 8th century BC, twins Romulus and Remus, fathered by the war god Mars, were born to the maiden, Rhea Silvia. Such was her shame that she hid the infants along the banks of a river. A she-wolf found the babes and suckled them, saving them from death. They were then discovered by shepherds and raised by them. The fable continues with the story that the adult Romulus slew his brother in a battle as to who should rule their tribe and founded the city of Rome on the Palatine Hill.

Below: *A representation of Romulus and Remus, Rome's founders.*

Pax Romana

In its heyday, at the death of **Emperor Hadrian** (AD117), the Roman Empire extended from today's Portugal to Damascus, and from Northumberland in northern England to the Nile in Egypt. It covered about 40 provinces (and touched on, by today's geography, some 40 different countries). Around 50 million people of many different races and religions lived in the vast Empire, a territory that embraced some half a dozen climatic zones. The conquered were absorbed into the Empire, made *cives Romani* (citizens of Rome) and, in some cases, rose to the enviable position of Emperor. Notable among these were **Trajan** and **Hadrian** (both from Spain) and **Septimius Severus** (from north Africa).

The Empire

On Caesar's death, Rome was thrust into civil war, which ended in 27BC when Octavian, assuming the name of **Augustus**, became the first elected emperor. He was one of Rome's greatest emperors and, for 41 years, the citizens lived in peace and thrived. Augustus was followed by a line of emperors of varying competence and sanity until the Hispanic citizen, **Trajan**, took charge in AD98, and his successor, **Hadrian**, reinforced the position of the Empire.

When Hadrian died in AD138, the Empire was never to attain such geographical or political prestige again. Under Diocletian (AD285–305), the Empire was divided into East and West, weakening its political clout. In AD306, **Constantine** became Emperor of a declining Rome and he legalized Christianity in AD313.

In the following two centuries, forces from the north of Europe made their presence felt. In AD476, Odoacer, king of the Goths, deposed Emperor Romulus Augustulus, bringing an end to the Western Empire.

The Dark Ages and Medieval Rome

The last centuries of the first millennium

were dark years for Rome. Christianity thrived, but conflict between political power and the power of the papacy became commonplace. The rivalry continued to simmer well into the 13th century. In 1417 the breach was healed and the Vatican became the papal residence.

Renaissance and Baroque

In the early 1500s, Catholicism was further challenged from the north as **Martin Luther** gained support and the Church irrevocably separated into two organizations with distinctly different doctrines. In 1527, Rome was sacked by the Holy Roman Emperor Charles V and many of its artistic treasures were lost. But thanks to many of the enlightened aristocracy who assumed the papacy through the 16th and 17th centuries, Rome recaptured some of its former architectural glory, and many of the city's elegant bridges, fountains, churches, convents and patrician palazzi date from these two centuries.

The 19th Century

In 1798, **Napoleon** captured Rome and declared it a republic. Some 10 years later, the French annexed the papal states, turning Rome into the second capital of the French Empire. Following Napoleon's downfall in 1815, Rome and the papal states were restored to the Pope, but a home-grown desire for Italian unification arose. In 1848, political unrest swept through the Italian peninsula and **Giuseppe Garibaldi** established a short-lived Roman republic the following year. The Pope fled but was reinstated by the French and Garibaldi returned to exile. Ten years later, Garibaldi supported the unification of Italy under the House of Piedmont, and his successful conquest of Sicily and Naples in 1860 enabled southern Italy to be united with the north under king **Victor Emmanuel II**. Unification was completed by the annexation of Venice in 1866 and then the papal states in 1870. In 1871, Rome finally became the capital of a united Italy.

Giuseppe Garibaldi

Garibaldi was largely responsible for uniting Italy in the 19th century. He lead a colourful life that started with a criminal record and ended with a seat as a deputy in parliament. Garibaldi fled Italy in 1834 when he was accused of taking part in a plot on the Genoese arsenal. He made his home in Latin America and became involved in the politics of **Brazil**, then **Uruguay** and **Argentina**. Returning to Italy in 1848, he grouped civilians in northern Italy and fought to liberate territory from the **French** and **Austrians**. Following another period of exile, he met up with Cavour and moved to unify the country under Vittorio Emanuele II, King of Savoy, championing Rome as the site of the country's capital. He is best remembered for taking **Sicily** and **Naples** with 1000 followers (the so-called 'Expedition of the Red Shirts') in 1860. In 1870, **Vittorio Emanuele II** became king of the first unified Italy and, in 1874, Garibaldi was elected deputy.

Opposite *A distinguished and fair ruler, Hadrian took the Empire to its largest extent.*

The 20th Century

In 1922, the fascist leader, **Benito Mussolini**, marched on Rome and assumed power. He orchestrated the 1929 signing of the **Lateran Treaty**, finally establishing peace between the government and the papacy. Papal jurisdiction was confined to the Vatican City and a few extra-territorial possessions, but the Church was given a vast sum of money in compensation and became a strong ally of the State.

Mussolini took Italy into World War II in 1940, but was executed in 1945 while trying to flee to Switzerland. At the end of the war, Victor Emmanuel III abdicated and although Umberto II took the throne, he lasted only until the following year when the Republic was re-proclaimed by a popular referendum. Umberto II and his family were exiled and took up residence in Switzerland. In 1957, Italy became one of the six founder members of the European Common Market – now the 25-strong European Union – by signing the **Treaty of Rome**.

The staging of the **Olympic Games** in 1960 was the highlight of a decade that deteriorated during the 1970s into political strife and terrorism attacks, which included the assassination of prime minister, Aldo Moro, by the **Red Brigade** in 1978. In the same year, **John Paul II** became the first non-Italian pope to be elected since 1522. After battling ill health for years, he died in 2005 and was succeeded by a German, who took the name of **Pope Benedict XVI**.

Benito Mussolini

Mussolini founded the Fascist Movement in 1919 and by 1924 held the majority of power in Italy. To garner lacking papal support, he signed the **Lateran Treaty** in 1929, then, in the 1930s (during the Spanish Civil War), aligned his party with **Franco**. In 1935, he invaded Ethiopia and, siding with Hitler, took Italy into World War II in 1940. Not all Italy was pro-Fascist and Mussolini executed many of those who turned against him, including his son-in-law. In 1943, **Il Duce** (as he was known) was deposed from within his party and interned in the **Abruzzi** only to be liberated by the Germans. On flight to neutral Switzerland after the Germans surrendered in 1945, he and his mistress, **Clara Petacci**, were lynched.

Government and Economy

Italy is a republic, with the president a ceremonial head of state holding office for a seven-year term. The prime minister heads the government, a position which he may hold for five years.

Despite being politically united for over 100 years, there remains in Italy a substantial north–south divide. Rome sits, more or less, on the divide and while it has its fair share of small industries, it is tourism in particular that brings revenue to the capital.

La Città del Vaticano (Vatican City)

The Head of State not only of the Vatican City but also of the Catholic Church worldwide, the **Pope** has absolute power in the Vatican. A **governor** is responsible for the administrative, judicial and economic services of the State. Revenues are gathered from **tourism**, **pilgrimages** and **donations**, enabling the Vatican to return a well-balanced account sheet each year.

The People

Italians are generally gregarious, excitable and passionate. Hedonists to the last, they will sacrifice much for the opportunity to dine and chat. In the last few decades, Rome has absorbed African and Asian immigrants and in some neighbourhoods the demographics have changed radically. The Italian spirit remains nevertheless enduring and those traditions, which attract the new resident or tourist to the country, are still upheld.

Roman Revenues
Until the 1970s, Rome relied on **tourism** and **agriculture** as its main sources of income. In the last quarter of the 20th century, however, it developed a whole new range of industries. The most lucrative are **mechanical construction**, **aeronautics** as well as **motorbike** and **scooter** manufacture. Its **electronics** industry has expanded, while refineries for both **chemicals** and **petroleum** have been built near Fiumicino. It also has an increasing **paper manufacturing** and **printing** sector.

Opposite: *The 16th-century palace, Palazzo di Montecitorio, became the seat of Italy's parliament early in the 20th century.*
Below: *Traffic police need to be particularly vigilent in congested central Rome.*

Below: *The Gothic chapel in Santa Maria sopra Minerva.*

Language

Latin, as spoken in Ancient Rome, has defined not only modern Italian but some six other languages too, and has given us our alphabet and structured English grammar. The Italian spoken today is similar to the language spoken 2000 years ago, but as a result of the increasing Americanization of Europe, the language has embraced some modernisms and Rome has evolved its own dialect and slang. Travellers who make the effort to learn some basic Italian will be met with warmth and enthusiasm, but those who don't, will no doubt find that their Roman hosts are quite competent in English!

Religion

Some 98 per cent of Italians are **Catholic**, but Rome also has a small percentage of **Jews**, **Protestants** and **Muslims**. Catholics celebrate all the traditional religious holidays, with particular reverence to **Christmas** and **Easter**.

Art and Architecture

Rome breathes history and art. No single civilization in Europe has left such an enduring mark on their lands and the civilizations that followed. Wherever you wander, modern Rome juxtaposes with the ancient city.

Rome has witnessed two truly great artistic periods. The first peaked with the height of the **Roman Empire**, around AD138, and the second was the **Baroque** age. Relics of the first period include the remains of various **Fora**, the **Colosseum**, the triumphal arches, the **Baths of Diocletian** and the **Pantheon**, as well as fabulous mosaics, frescoes and breathtaking sculptures.

From early Medieval days, there is **Santa Maria sopra Minerva**, the only extant Gothic church in Rome, and the beautiful apse mosaics in **Santa Maria** in **Trastevere** and **Santa Maria Maggiore**.

In the 14th century the popes did much to redress the importance of the city. The building of St Peter's was begun, and Sixtus IV commissioned the **Sistine Chapel**, decorated later by **Michelangelo**.

Baroque reached its purest form in Rome and this was an era of great religious architecture. Post-Baroque Rome is not devoid of buildings, but there is little of outstanding merit.

Above: *The Ponto Rotto (Broken Bridge) dates back to the 2nd century BC.*

Film

A number of the darker landmarks of 20th-century cinema came out of Italy. This was where **neorealism** started, with such young film-makers as **Rossellini** and **De Sica**. For a while, the studios were courted by international film makers, and the epics *Ben Hur* and *Spartacus* were made here. A few note-worthy Italian directors include Federico **Fellini**, Bernardo **Bertolucci** and Pier Paolo **Pasolini** who all became household names. A few great films were made in the 1980s – *The Last Emperor* by Bertolucci and *Cinema Paradiso* by Tornatore – but the film studios were waning as the new breed of realism took hold. The runaway hit *La Vita è Bella* by Roberto Benigni has done much to improve the fortunes of the movie industry. Rome is a popular centre for TV work and Scorcese filmed *Gangs of New York* here in 2001.

Federico Fellini
One of Italy's foremost film directors, Fellini was born in Rimini, on the east coast of Italy. He soon gravitated to Rome and collaborated on the film scripts of a number of lesser movies. He made his first film, *Luci del Varietà*, in 1950 and, during the course of his life, wrote and directed 24 films. Amongst these were the classics, *La Strada* (1954), *La Dolce Vita* (1959), *Otto e Mezzo* (1963) and *Satyricon* (1969), all of which had a profound effect on Italian cinema. His later works never received the same acclaim as these early films. He died in Rome in 1993.

The Fora

Originally marshland between Rome's seven hills, this zone became the meeting and trading point between the various groups that inhabited the hills during the 1st millennium BC. The Fora – actually a series of successive Fora built by the first rulers – are so ruined and intermixed that it is hard to get a clear grasp of their layout. They are best seen, at first, from the **Capitoline Hill**. Today's broad avenue, **Via dei Fori Imperiali** that runs from Piazza Venezia to the Colosseum, divides the Fora. The **Roman Forum** (the most important of the sites) lies to the south and the **Fori Imperiali** lie to its north.

Below: *The Temple of Vesta now has but three columns.*

◎ *See* Map C–B1   ★★★

ROMAN FORUM

The **Sacra Via**, which runs through the centre of this ancient forum, served as a processional route taken by victorious generals. It leads from the 4th-century **Arch of Constantine** via the imposing **Arch of Titus**, built in AD81 by Domitian in memory of his brother, into the heart of the Roman Forum.

On the right are the remains of the large **Temple of Venus and Rome**, built in AD135 by Hadrian who may also have designed it. The elegant, slim **Temple of Antoninus and Faustina** was erected in AD141 by Antoninus Pius in memory of his wife, Faustina, and also shelters an 11th-century church, San Lorenzo.

Reflect for a moment at the **Temple of Caesar**, on the spot where Caesar was cremated and Mark Anthony made his funerary oration. Sometimes, there are small offerings of flowers to the far-from-forgotten ruler. The circular **Temple of Vesta**, rebuilt in AD191, was where the sacred flame – the synonym for the continuation of the Roman state – was kept. Nearby, the three remaining columns from the **Temple of the Dioscuri**, part of the cult of Castor and Pollux, are all that are left of the original 484BC temple.

Judging by the seven remaining columns, the **Temple of Saturn**, consecrated in 498BC but rebuilt in 42BC, must have been huge, towering over the beautiful **Arch of Septimius Severus**, built in AD203 and dedicated to the former emperor by his son, Caracalla. Look out for the **Curia**, where the Roman Senate used to meet, and the remaining Corinthian columns of the **Temple of Vespasian and Titus**.

See Map C–C1 | ★★★

THE COLOSSEUM

Seventy-six numbered entrances and four VIP entrances lead into this huge elliptical amphitheatre commissioned by the greatest Flavian emperor, **Vespasian**. It came to be known as the Colosseum, it is believed, because of the colossal bronze statue of **Nero** that once stood nearby. Capable of holding up to 85,000 spectators, the building witnessed some of the bloodiest combats in the history of the Empire.

Gladiatorial combats continued until AD407, and fights with wild beasts until AD422 when Christianity, and its values, began to take hold on a declining Rome. These marathon spectacles were staged by the Emperor and his elite and were open to all, free of charge.

Below the arena, a labyrinth of corridors and rooms housed machinery, men and beasts. Over this a wooden floor was laid, topped with sand (to prevent combatants from slipping and to absorb the blood). The entire area was covered by a vellum roof, which was secured to posts around the circumference, and remains of these still exist. Along the ground level, and under the seating, was the *vomitorium* where ablutions took place.

Today, it is possible to visit most parts of the Colosseum. Guided evening tours are offered twice weekly in summer months.

Above: *Much damaged by pollution, the rear of the Colosseum rises to its original four storeys.*

The Colosseum
✉ Via Celio Vibenna
🕐 Open daily
09:00–17:00
☎ 06 3996-7700
🖳 www.pierreci.it –
reservation includes
free audio guide
M Colosseo
💰 €9 + €2 for exhibitions – ticket valid for the Palatine walkway

---

Gladiatorial Games
To escape death, combatants had to fell their adversary, or a wounded gladiator could entrust his fate to the Emperor. The Colosseum was inaugurated with a three-month orgy of death; some 2000 gladiators lost their lives.

Above: *Part of the Roman mosaic in the Palazzo Massimo, showing hippos.*

⊙ *See* Map D–C5	★★★

PALAZZO MASSIMO

In 1998, many of the priceless exhibits from the **Museo Nazionale Romano** were moved to the beautifully renovated Palazzo Massimo, diagonally across Piazza del Cinquecento; others remain in the **Diocletian Baths** while a further collection is housed in the **Palazzo Altemps** (*see* page 36).

This collection of Roman sculpture, wall painting, mosaics, early jewellery and coins is one of the most exciting and accessible in the city and constitutes one of Italy's most important collections.

Pride of the museum is the extraordinarily beautiful reconstructed room from **Livia's House**, a dining room painted to recreate the countryside, complete with birds, plants and flowers. On the same floor is the interior of an ancient Roman villa found in the grounds of **Villa Farnesina** (*see* page 36). The pitch-black room is decorated with sublime small, coloured paintings of mythological scenes and landscapes linked by painted festoons. Nearby is the collection of magnificent mosaics, some so delicate they seem more like paintings; these once formed the floors of patrician homes. Book ahead on timed tickets to see the frescoes. A fine series of low-relief sculptures from the 2nd century AD depict the costumes of Roman *cives* in different parts of the Empire. Also on the ground floor are scores of Greek, and copies of Greek, sculptural masterpieces. Many of the sculptures found at Hadrian's Villa in Tivoli are now housed here.

Palazzo Massimo
⊠ piazza dei Cinquecento 67
🕘 Open daily 09:00–20:00
☎ 06 4890-3500
M Termini
💰 €6.50

Face to Face with the Famous
The collection of ancient busts in Palazzo Massimo is fascinating. Beautifully displayed, you can take stock of **Caligula**, Nero's wife, **Poppea**, **Vespasian**, **Hadrian**, **Marcus Aurelius**, **Septimius Severus** or **Caracalla**. It is a good opportunity to get to grips with the complex chronology of the Roman emperors and their immediate families.

THE PANTHEON

One of Rome's most extraordinary buildings, the Pantheon (which in Greek means 'all the gods') has been a place of worship for some 2000 years. It was originally constructed by **Marcus Agrippa** around 27BC as a temple of pagan worship but was later destroyed by fire and replaced by Hadrian, the great emperor-architect. At the beginning of the 7th century, it was consecrated by Pope Bonifacio IV as a place of Christian worship and has remained so to this day.

Circular, with a coffered dome, the magnificent Pantheon rises to a height of 43.3m (142ft) and is the same height as the width of the building – in fact, a vertical section of its plan forms a perfect circle. In the centre of the dome, an oculus of some nine metres (30ft) remains open to the elements. Sunlight streams in during summer, illuminating the multi-coloured marble floor and elegant lower walls, while showers fall unhindered in winter.

Around the walls are three tombs of note, those of Italy's first king, **Vittorio Emanuele II**, his queen, **Margherita**, and the artist, **Raphael**, who requested his interment in the building.

The Pantheon
✉ Piazza della Rotunda
🕐 08:30–19:30
Mon–Sat; 09:00–18:00
Sun; 09:00–13:00 holidays; 09:00–17:00
Mass Saturday;
09:00–10:30 Mass
Sunday.
☎ 06 6830-0230
Ⓜ Spagna or Colosseo
💲 Free
♿ Disabled access

Below: *The beautifully proportioned façade of the Pantheon is the focal point for many tourists taking a breather over coffee or cocktails.*

Palazzo Doria Pamphilj
✉ piazza della Collegio Romano 2
🕐 10:00–17:00; closed Thursday
☎ 06 679-7323
🖥 www.doriapamphilj.it
M Barberini, Spagna or Colosseo (better to take the bus 64/60 to Piazza Venezia)
💰 €8
♿ Disabled access

Piazza Navona
M Spagna

See Map D–D5   ★★★

PALAZZO DORIA PAMPHILJ

One of Rome's most important art galleries, the **Doria Pamphilj Collection** is a privately owned gallery of paintings and sculpture accumulated by two great families who intermarried. Their story is told on the portable information cassettes, narrated by the current prince.

Among the many paintings that crowd the walls are some real masterpieces, but don't just gaze at the exhibits: the various salons and the chapel are wonderful works of art too.

Be sure to look out for **Velázquez's** portrait of *Innocent X* (a member of the Pamphilj family), landscapes by **Claude Lorrain**, religious subjects by **Annibale Carracci**, two **Caravaggio** paintings – *Rest on the Flight into Egypt*, with its striking back view of the angel musician, and *The Penitent Magdalene*, echoing the pose of Mary in the previous painting – a *Deposition* by **Hans Memlinc**, and various paintings by the Dutch master, **Jan Brueghel the Elder**. There are also some **Gobelin** tapestries.

Below: *Palazzo Doria Pamphilj is still owned by the Doria Pamphilj family.*

Wander onwards, through the **Piazza del Collegio Romano**, and beyond the **Palazzo del Collegio Romano**, which was formerly the site of a Jesuit college. Take the Via Sant'Ignazio to the piazza of the same name.

See Map D–C5 | ★★★

PIAZZA NAVONA

Once the **Stadium of Domitian**, this elegant, elongated 'square' is one of Rome's favourite places for relaxation, dining and people-watching. The 16th-century palaces rising from the perimeter of the piazza were constructed around the central part of the stadium and comprise some extremely impressive buildings, many of which have been recently renovated.

Above: *The centre of the Baroque Fontana di Nettuno, Piazza Navona.*

But it is the fountains that hold the focus of this piazza. Pride of place goes to the central **Fontana dei Quattro Fiumi**, commissioned by Innocent X (whose Palazzo Pamphilj occupies a large frontage nearby). It is a gushing fountain surrounding an Egyptian obelisk and, with its colossal statues, fêtes the four greatest rivers known at that time – the Danube, Ganges, Nile and Plate. Bernini designed this Baroque splendour with characteristic vigour and it was completed by his assistants in 1651. At the southern end of the piazza is the **Fontana del Moro** by Giacomo della Porta and, at the northern end, the **Fontana di Nettuno**, where Neptune struggles with a recalcitrant monster of the deep amid a turbulence of sea horses, is by Antonio della Bitta.

> **Don't Believe the Stories**
> Guides love to fabricate myths around facts. Stories of the rivalry between **Bernini** and **Borromini** abound. Rivalry did exist, but there is absolutely no truth in the story that the figure of the Nile in Bernini's **Fontana dei Quattro Fiumi** is shielding his eyes from seeing Borromini's Sant'Agnese. Bernini finished the sculpture in 1651, two years before Borromini began the church.

See Map D–E3 ★★★

PIAZZA DI SPAGNA

One of the most famous tourist spots in Rome, the largely pedestrian piazza and the flight of steps behind it are named after the 17th-century **Palazzo di Spagna**, which is the residence of the Spanish Ambassador to the Vatican located on the west side of the piazza, and indeed notable for being the first permanent ambassadorial residence in Rome.

This lovely piazza not only offers beautiful Roman buildings and a boat-shaped fountain designed by Bernini, but

Above: *Bernini designed this unusual fountain in the Piazza di Spagna.*

a magnificent sweep of 137 stairs, the **Scalinata di Trinità dei Monti**, leading up to an attractive Baroque church, **Trinità dei Monti** (*see* page 34).

On each side of the Spanish Steps, small apartments with matchbox terraces and exuberant little gardens jostle for space. Horses and buggies, flower sellers and milling visitors from all parts of the world kindle a festive, cosmopolitan atmosphere. The beauty of this part of Rome was not lost on travellers – artists and writers in the 18th and 19th centuries and many foreigners made it their temporary home.

Piazza di Spagna
M Spagna

Palazzo di Spagna
🕐 09:00–17:00; closed Monday
☎ 06 678-4351/2
M Spagna
♿ Varies

See Map D–C3   ★★★

ARA PACIS (ALTAR OF PEACE)

The Ara Pacis (Altar of Peace) has been reconstructed, renovated and enclosed in a glassy new museum designed by Richard Meier. Its solid white marble form positively glistens. The monument was erected in AD13 to commemorate the peace Rome enjoyed as a result of **Augustus**'s successful incorporation of Gaul and Spain into the Empire. It comprises three walls on a dais, reached by a flight of steps, enclosing an altar used annually for an anniversary sacrifice. All the external walls are carved with decorative foliage, and exquisite and extraordinarily lifelike scenes of people, including an array of members of the emperor's family – it has, in today's terms, the realism of a family photograph.

Ara Pacis
⊠ Lungotevere in Augusta
⊕ Closed Monday and public holidays;
Tue–Sun 09:00–19:00;
Christmas Eve and New Year's Day 09:00–14:00
☎ 06 8205-9127
🖳 www.arapacis.it
M Flaminio
🔊 €6.50 – guided visits on request

Augustus's Legacy
Augustus was one of Rome's great emperors. He applied rules of civic building and did much to beautify the city, leaving a report when he died in AD14 in which he stated, 'I was born to a city of brick and left a city of marble.' Along the banks of the Tiber, and in an area forgotten by commerce, lies the ruined **Mausoleo di Augusto** (Augustus's Mausoleum), one of the great legacies of Ancient Rome. Magnificent on its completion in 28BC, Augustus's circular mausoleum today remains as a weed-covered mound, surrounded by funereal cypress trees, and is mainly used by local dogs and joggers. Access to the monument itself is by appointment only.

Left: *The fine details sculpted on the Ara Pacis.*

See Map A & B ★★★

St Peter's Basilica and Square
✉ Piazza San Pietro
🕐 Apr–Sep
07:00–19:00; Oct–Mar
07:00–18:00;
Treasury: Apr–Sep
09:00–18:00; Oct–Mar
09:00–17:30;
Grottoes: Apr–Sep
07:00–19:00; Oct–Mar
07:00–17:00; **Cupola:**
Apr–Sep 08:00–18:00;
Oct–Mar 08:00–16:45
☎ 011 3906-6982
📠 06 6988-5100
M Ottaviano-San Pietro
💰 €13 – includes
Vatican museums and
Sistine Chapel

Museo Storico Artistico
🕐 Open daily
09:00–10:00 and
11:00–12:00
💰 €4

Below: *The magnificent façade of St Peter's Basilica dazzles again after its recent facelift.*

ST PETER'S BASILICA AND SQUARE

The largest basilica in Christendom, with a magnificent colonnaded piazza in front, St Peter's is undoubtedly one of the most impressive sights in Italy. It is not, however, the mother church of the faith; that title is reserved by San Giovanni in Laterano. The façade of St Peter's is best admired from the 20th-century thoroughfare – the **Via della Conciliazione** – leading to the Tiber, while the views of Rome and the piazza are breathtaking from the bird's-eye viewpoint, high up outside St Peter's dome.

A basilica was first erected by Constantine in the mid-4th century AD on the spot where St Peter was buried. Most of the basilica, however, is the result of Julius II's commissioning **Bramante** as architect in 1503 to redesign the edifice, and the building's subsequent continuation under **Michelangelo** in the mid-16th century. He was responsible for the dome and the rear of the basilica, and in 1626 **Maderno** added a nave and façade. The postscript, the piazza – its circular form taken from Nero and Caligula's circus, which lies beneath – was the brainchild of **Bernini**, whose finishing touches were only completed between 1656 and 1667. It is a wonder that with such a number of artists

See Map A & B ★★★

and the length of time taken to complete it, the building achieves such majesty and harmony.

Not to be missed in the basilica are Michelangelo's intriguingly delicate *Pietà*, now behind protective glass; Bernini's **baldacchino**, made from bronze stripped from the Pantheon, its barley-sugar columns sheltering the high altar used by the Pope – and only the Pope – to celebrate mass; and high above, the light, airy and beautifully decorated dome designed by Michelangelo but finished only after his death. Below the Basilica there are the crypts, with the **Tomb of St Peter**.

Among the other sculptural masterpieces are the grandiose **Monument to Pope Alexander VII** by Bernini, and the gaunt figure of St Peter, attributed to the 13th-century architect and sculptor **Arnolfo di Cambio**, its big toe polished by generations of pilgrims kissing it. Before leaving the building, take the time to look at the considerable treasures forming the **Museo Storico Artistico** next to the **Sacristy**.

To the right of the main basilica is the lift up to the main roof and portico. If you wish to climb the dome, it is a couple of hundred steps more from here. Many visitors stay in the pleasant Borgo area directly to the north of the Vatican, traditionally where pilgrims stayed in the Middle Ages.

The Pope gives a blessing to the crowd in the piazza every Sunday at noon, if he is in Rome.

Above: *From most parts of Rome, the dome of St Peter's Basilica is visible.*

Wednesday Papal Audience
Visitors who would like to see the Pope should apply to the Prefetto della Casa Pontificia, ✉ Città del Vaticano, 00120, Rome, ☎ 06 6982. Apply ahead of time in writing, or the Monday beforehand in person at the office to the right of St Peter's.

Surprising Statistics
St Peter's Basilica can accommodate 60,000 worshippers. It took 170 years to build during the reign of 24 different popes, and it used to take nearly 2000 individuals to light the 5991 lamps and lanterns around the building.

See Map A–B2 | ★★★

Above: *A magnificent artistic achievement, the Sistine Chapel is worth the long queues to enter the Vatican.*

THE SISTINE CHAPEL

One of man's greatest artistic achievements, the Sistine Chapel was rebuilt as the official private chapel of the popes by Pope Sixtus IV in the 1470s. It was his nephew, Pope Julius II, who subsequently commissioned the talented Michelangelo to paint the famous ceiling, and Pope Paul III who commissioned his powerful *Last Judgment* on the wall behind the great altar. But the marvels do not rest there. The lower walls, too, are beautifully painted by other great Renaissance artists. The Sistine Chapel is also where the **Sacred College of Cardinals** meet when electing a new Pope.

The Ceiling

Since its historic cleaning by the Japanese and its opening again to the public in the 1990s, the now colourful, barrel-vaulted ceiling of the Sistine Chapel has drawn much debate.

Michelangelo shunned all cooperation when he accepted the huge commission and, between 1508 and 1512, worked entirely on his own, often splayed on his back high up on a specially built scaffolding that, it appears, was suspended from the walls rather than resting on the floor.

The 33 frescoes, painted on the curving ceiling between pilasters and supports, depict scenes from the Old Testament, interspersed with large Sibyls (ancient prophet-

The Sistine Chapel
✉ Piazza San Pietro
🕐 Apr–Sep
07:00–19:00; Oct–Mar
07:00–18:00
📞 06 6988-5100
Ⓜ Ottaviano-San Pietro

⭐ *See* Map A–B2   ★★★

esses) and nude athletes all set in a painted architectural backdrop. These massive forms, often muscular and masculine, sometimes swathed in flowing attire and sometimes entirely derobed, are almost all hymns to the human body (indeed, the nudity in Michelangelo's *Last Judgment* was later painted over by order of Pius IV). Among the best known scenes are the **Creation of Adam**, where the hand of God reaches out to Man; the *Temptation and Expulsion from Paradise*; and the *Delphic Sibyl*, whose face is unusually tender and beautiful.

The Last Judgment

This wall fresco rises with frightening intensity behind the great altar and boldly outlines the horrors that await sinners after death. Commissioned by the Farnese pope, **Paul III**, it represents the last great, large-scale work by Michelangelo who died in 1545, four years after its completion. All the saints are depicted here, along with Christ – a simple, beardless figure – against the clear lapis lazuli blue sky. There are several contemporary portraits, too, among the personages.

The Walls

Below Michelangelo's œuvre are the 12 large wall panels frescoed between 1481 and 1483 by such artists as Perugino (Raphael's master), Pinturicchio, Ghirlandaio, Rosselli and Signorelli. The individual panels show scenes from the life of Moses (on the right facing the altar) and the life of Christ. It is worth lingering here for these paintings are also masterpieces of Renaissance art.

Picking a Pope

The position as Bishop of Rome and head of the Roman Catholic Church is lifelong for the Pope. Upon his death, all members of the Sacred College of Cardinals below the age of 80 are confined in the Sistine Chapel until the new Pope is decided upon. They meet twice daily to vote and, by tradition, release a stream of smoke from the chimney vent above the Sistine Chapel to communicate the status of their conclave. Black smoke indicates that the cardinals have not yet decided, while white smoke announces the election of a new Pope.

> **Villa Borghese and Galleria Borghese**
> ✉ piazzale Scipione Borghese 5
> 🕐 Tue–Sun 09:00–19:00
> ☎ 06 841-3979
> 🎟 €8.50

⊙ *See* Map D–E1   ★★★

VILLA BORGHESE

Scipione Borghese, nephew of Pope Paul V, commissioned the Villa Borghese in 1605. It was modified over the following two centuries and passed into the hands of the State in 1903. Shaded in parts by centuries-old trees, the park has an artificial lake, statues, imitation Classical temples and a zoo.

The ground floor of the villa, the **Borghese Museum**, is a vast repository of sculpture dating from the Greeks to the Romans, and from the 17th to the 19th centuries. Among the most impressive Classical pieces are the *Sleeping Hermaphrodite*, a Roman copy of the famous Greek sculpture; Canova's *Pauline Borghese*, a beautiful nude; Bernini's *Apollo and Daphne*, a sublime marble rendition of the two gods as Daphne morphs into a tree; and Bernini's *David*, reputed to be a self-portrait.

> **On Caravaggio's Trail**
> **Galleria Borghese** boasts a fine collection of the master's works. Among the most impressive is the *Giovane con la canestra di frutta*, a beautiful and youthful work. His *Bacchino malato*, the portrait of a young man as Bacchus, by contrast reflects his ill health after being hospitalized.

The **Galleria Borghese**, on the first floor, is rich with painted masterpieces, and the rooms are beautifully decorated. Look out for **Raphael's** *Deposition*, *Lady with a Unicorn* and the *Portrait of Pope Julius II*, his great patron. There are some excellent works by **Caravaggio**, including the *Young Man with a Basket of Fruit* and *St John the Baptist*. Andrea del Sarto's *Madonna and Child with the Infant St John* is a fine example of this talented artist's extraordinary skills.

See Map D–C5   ★★

PIAZZA CAMPO DE' FIORI

In one of the older parts of Rome, hidden in a maze of narrow, winding streets, lies the popular 'square', Piazza Campo de' Fiori. An elongated piazza that was once a meadow (hence its name, 'Field of Flowers') and then one of Rome's most important squares, it is known

today for its brightly coloured **morning market** (the mosaic of colourful, clean vegetables, flowers and fruit is a wonderful sight), has a peaceful, laid-back air about it and, despite the number of tourists, breathes 'Real Rome'.

A central position in the square is occupied by the brooding statue of a hooded **Giordano Bruno**, a 'heretic' burned alive by the Inquisition in 1600 – a sobering reminder that this was the site where many others lost their lives.

Campo de' Fiori is largely pedestrian (although not off-limits to motorbikes). On Sundays and weekday afternoons – when the market has closed – Campo de' Fiori provides a fine place to stroll, stop for a cappuccino or *aperitivo*, or linger over a leisurely pasta lunch or dinner. In the small streets on each side of the piazza there are scores of cafés, restaurants and popular *trattorie*; the shops here have a genuine neighbourhood quality to them and prices are much more realistic than those in the most popular tourist spots.

Above: *Early risers get the pick of the crop in Campo de' Fiori's market.*
Opposite: *The beautiful park at Villa Borghese is a perfect place to relax after a long day of sightseeing.*

Campo de' Fiori's Market
✉ Piazza Campo de' Fiori
⊕ Closed Sunday

☉ See Map D–D5 & Map F | ★★

Above: *Filippino Lippi's magnificent altarpiece depicting St Thomas Aquinas presenting Cardinal Carafa to the Virgin, part of the Carafa Chapel.*

SANTA MARIA SOPRA MINERVA

If you backtrack through Via Sant'Ignazio and along Via Pie d' Marmo – where a large Roman foot is the highlight – you will arrive in Piazza della Minerva. With an obelisk borne on the back of an elaborately carved marble elephant (a Bernini folly), the mostly pedestrian square is dominated on one side by the church of **Santa Maria sopra Minerva**.

An old church of immense artistic interest, Santa Maria sopra Minerva has a rather dreary façade but the interior of the church is a delight. Its restoration has, to some people's taste, over-emphasized the gilt and colour but the effect is nevertheless impressive. Be sure to look up at the star-studded blue ceiling, and note how the light streams through the clerestory windows to pattern the lovely marble floor.

Two side chapels deserve a visit: the **Cappella Carafa**, donated by Cardinal Olivieri Carafa and decorated with frescoes and paintings by Florentine artist, **Filippino Lippi**, and the chapel designed by **Carlo Maderno**, with an altarpiece of *The Annunciation* by Antoniazzo Romano. There is also a fresco by Merlozzo da Forlì on the opposite side of the church.

Santa Maria sopra Minerva
✉ piazza della Minerva 42
🕘 09:00–19:00; Chapels 08:00–13:00 and 15:50–19:30
Ⓜ Bus 64 from Termini station. Stop at Largo Argentina.

☆ See Map D–D3   ★★

VIA CONDOTTI

If there is one area dedicated to shopping and the purchase of all that is *alta moda*, it is this zone between Via del Corso and Piazza di Spagna. The names of the streets are synonyms for high fashion – Via Frattini, Via Borgognona and **Via Condotti** – and if you want to gauge the state of Italian fashion, this is the best place to indulge yourself.

Milling between the different stores, *caffès* and restaurants are the best-dressed women (and men) in Rome, toting designer shopping bags and mobile phones, as well as motley-clad tourists strolling from one fine window display to the next.

The names that made Italy so big on the fashion scene – **Armani**, **Benetton**, **Gucci**, **Laura Biagiotti**, **Fendi**, **Valentino** and **Versace** – may all be found in this golden rectangle. In their midst is **Modigliani**, known for its superb collection of household ware, with a fine range of porcelain and glass from the world's best producers.

At via Condotti 86, there is an institution of a different sort: **Caffè Greco**, a café that has remained popular since its Greek owner opened it in 1760. Its coffee-drinking patrons through the ages include **Goethe** (who lived just down the road, at via del Corso 18), **Byron**, **Keats**, **Berlioz**, **Wagner** and **Baudelaire**. Today, it is frequented as much by Romans as by foreigners intent on immersing themselves in the charming atmosphere of this historic hostelry.

Via Condotti
M Spagna

Modigliani
✉ via Frattina 87
☎ 06 679-1082

Caffè Greco
✉ via Condotti 86
☎ 06 679-1700

Below: *Via Condotti is known for its pricey shops.*

See Map E–F3 | ★★

Hadrian's Villa
✉ Via di Villa Adriana Tivoli
🕐 Open daily 08:30–18:00
☎ 06 3996-7900
Ⓜ Ponte Mamolo, then bus in direction of Via Prenestina
♿ €6.50

Emperor Hadrian
Adriano was born in the Roman town of Italica, on the outskirts of what is today Seville. In AD117, Hadrian was crowned Emperor in Rome and ruled until his death in AD138. Hadrian was a great builder and talented amateur architect. He is reputed to have designed the Temple of Venus and Rome.

HADRIAN'S VILLA

Heading out from Rome along the Via Tiburtina, the highway rises into the **Sabine Hills** which are just 31km (20 miles) from the city, where the small and rather un-attractive town of Tivoli is situated. Since the days of the Republic it has been popu-lar with Roman citizens escaping the claw-ing summer heat and taking the sul-phurous waters in its springs.

It was at the foot of the Sabine Hills that Emperor Hadrian chose in AD118 to site his Villa, a large residential and recre-ational complex of which little remains intact today. It requires imagination – and stamina – to take in the 120ha (300-acre) site. Many of the sculptures are now in Roman museums.

A scale model at the entrance gives an idea of the Villa's former glory. Of particular interest are the **Smaller Baths**, the large replica of the Athenian Stoa Poikile, now just a grassy arena, the **Canopus**, a beauti-ful artificial pool sur-rounded by caryatids and columns which was inspired by the famous sanctuary at Serapis, Egypt, and the so-called **Maritime Theatre**, a circular pool with a central island that was probably a private retreat for Hadrian.

See Map D–E4 | ★

FONTANA DI TREVI

To ensure that you will return to Rome, so they say, toss a coin over your opposite shoulder and into the fountain. Toss two to meet a Roman, toss three for marriage. It's such enduring folklore – and the wonderful Baroque sculpture – that bring the crowds to **Trevi Fountain**. The sound of tumbling water fills the air, couples pose for photographs and souvenir salesmen fare well. There are quiet corners around the fountain filled with cafés, ideal for a quick reviver. Dominating the piazza of the same name, **Neptune**, god of the sea, bursts from an elaborate Baroque façade, while two tritons tussle with sea creatures. It was built for Pope Clement XII by Nicolo Salvi in 1762 at the point where the Aqua Vergine, ancient Rome's main aqueduct, ended.

While walking back down **Via delle Muratte**, look at the 20th-century building (an office and apartment block) on the left, where every surface of its courtyard is decorated with paintings and designs.

Above: *Completed in 1762, the Fontana di Trevi is one of the capital's most elaborate fountains.*
Opposite: *Part of the Canopus, at Hadrian's Villa.*

Fontana di Trevi
M Barberini
There are a number of excellent restaurants situated around the Fountain area.

See Map G–B2 ★

Santa Maria in Trastevere
✉ Piazza Santa Maria in Trastevere
☎ 06 581-4802
🕐 Open daily 07:30–20:00
💰 Free

SANTA MARIA IN TRASTEVERE

In the heart of Trastevere, in the piazza of the same name, lies this popular basilica. Its colonnaded entrance, designed by Carlo Fontana in 1702, and 12th-century *campanile* sit tightly between 18th-century *palazzi*. Carlo Fontana's octagonal fountain in the middle of the piazza has become a gathering point for the itinerant, and unfortunately their ménage does little to enhance the piazza's intrinsic charm.

Santa Maria's origins go back to early Christian times but its form today is largely Medieval. It was reconstructed in 1140 on orders from **Pope Innocent II**, incorporating many granite columns pilfered from ancient Roman buildings. The mosaic work on the floor is a later remodelling in the Cosmati style.

The basilica is a favourite one for marriages, such is its unique and beautiful atmosphere. Above the high altar, the magnificent 13th-century mosaics – including the *Coronation of the Virgin* and a series of mosaics by **Pietro Cavallini** depicting the *Life of the Virgin* – shine in the subdued light. The narrow roads leading off the central piazza are full of small restaurants, their tables and parasols spilling onto the streets.

Below: *Beneath the superb Medieval mosaics, the nave of Santa Maria in Trastevere is formed with Classical columns.*

✿ *See* Map G	★

TRASTEVERE

Although Trastevere has few sites to tempt the tourist – there are no Classical antiquities, although there are a handful of interesting Medieval churches with exquisite frescoes – the real attraction lies not in these but in Trastevere's Roman ambience. For, in the shadow of the Janiculum, it comprises a neighbourhood of narrow, cobbled streets that breathes character. Life is played out on the streets, music tumbles out through open windows into its alleys, and washing lines string together the sienna and ochre buildings. It has become very fashionable to live in Trastevere, to dine within its ancient walls, and many are the small family *trattorie* that spill out onto the pretty passageways. With its plethora of bars and clubs, Trastevere has also gained a reputation with the social set as one of Rome's popular nightspots.

Start with an *aperitivo* and some people-watching at Caffè di Marzio or Caffè delle Arance, both in Piazza Santa Maria; you may even find a concert in the church opposite. Perhaps a good glass of wine would be in order; wander over to wine bar Uva Rara, next to the popular restaurant Il Pastarellaro – or end the evening with an ice at Fonte della Salute, via Cardinale Marmaggi 2–4.

Below: *Trastevere is probably Rome's most colourful quarter. Not only are the narrow streets clogged with cars and motorbikes, but buildings are painted warm earthy colours, the streets are decorated with trailing plants and decked out with lines of washing.*

Santa Maria in Cosmedin

Renowned for its splendid Medieval mosaics, this ancient church (✉ Bocca della Verità 18) is smallish, plain and rather dark. Towering above Santa Maria is a tall seven-storey bell tower dating from the church's rebuilding in 1123. The church has unusually thin columns along the nave, wonderful stonework on the floor, a fine Gothic *baldacchino* created by one of the Cosmati sons and, probably its greatest asset, a low-relief sculpted human face set in the wall. Its mouth – a gaping hole, known as the **Bocca della Verità** (Mouth of Truth) – attracts tourists by the hundreds who place their hands inside and pose for photos. Originally, it was used as a 'litmus test' for suspects who believed, if they lied, the mouth would close.

Churches
San Clemente Papa al Laterano

Quirky church with fine floor mosaics. Real attraction is to descend to the bowels of the building to discover the remains of the previous churches.
✉ *Via San Giovanni in Laterano* ☎ *06 774-0021* ⏰ *09:00–12:00, 15:00–18:00 (summer months open at 10:00)*

Sant'Andrea al Quirinale

The plain, yellow façade belies the richness of the interior. This Bernini-designed church is a gem.
✉ *via del Quirinale 29*
☎ *06 474-4872*
⏰ *08:00–12:00, 16:00–19:00. Closed Tuesday.*

San Carlino alle Quattro Fontane

One of artist Borromini's greatest works. With its series of concave and convex walls, oval dome and light stucco, the interior seems larger than on plan.
✉ *via del Quirinale 23*

☎ *06 488-3261*
⏰ *10:00–13:00, Sun 12:00–13:00, 15:00–17:30. Closed Saturday.*

La Chiesa del Gesù

The first Jesuit church built in Rome. An elaborate masterpiece with beautifully decorated columns, pilasters, walls, ceiling and cupola.
✉ *Piazza del Gesù*
☎ *06 697-001*
⏰ *check website: www.chiesadelgesu.org*

Sant'Eligio degli Orefici

Designed by Raphael (though finished by Peruzzi) this small but beautiful church is built on the form of a Greek cross with a cupola.
✉ *via Sant'Eligio 8*
☎ *06 686-8260*
⏰ *Closed Wed and weekends; 10:00–13:00 all other days.*

Trinità dei Monti

This twin-towered church commands a magnificent position overlooking southwest Rome. Among

the points of interest are the side chapels decorated with Mannerist works – *The Assumption* by Daniele da Volterra is a real masterpiece.
✉ *Piazza Trinità dei Monti* ☎ *06 679-2245* ⏱ *09:00–13:00, 15:00–19:00*

Santa Cecilia in Trastevere

Peaceful church with 9th-century apse mosaic, impressive altar canopy and 13th-century fresco remains of the *Last Judgment.*
✉ *piazza Santa Cecilia 22* ☎ *06 589-9289* ⏱ *10:00–12:00, 16:00–18:00*

San Pietro in Montorio

Erected on the presumed site of St Peter's crucifixion, this church is decorated by works of some of the Renaissance's great masters.
✉ *Piazza San Pietro in Montorio* ☎ *06 581-3940* ⏱ *09:00–12:00, 16:00–18:00*

Historical Buildings
Palazzo del Quirinale

In one of Rome's smartest areas, this stately building, once the summer residence of the 16th-century popes, became the residence of the kings of Italy. It is now the official residence and office of the president.
✉ *Piazza del Quirinale* ☎ *06 46991* ⏱ *Sunday 08:30–12:00* ♿ €5

Palazzo Nuovo

Renowned for its collection of Classical sculpture, here you will gain some understanding of the great achievements of Classical Greece and

Opposite: *Rome's beautiful churches host a continual stream of weddings.* **Below:** *The vivid colours of the Palazzo del Quirinale distinguish the official residence of Italy's state president.*

Chiesa Nuova

Chiesa Nuova, or **Santa Maria in Vallicella** – to give it its correct name – is an interesting building on **Piazza Chiesa Nuova**, attached to the **Oratorio dei Filippini**. Their brilliant white façades shine out through the polluted surrounds. Built as the centre of Filippo Neri's new order, the Fathers of the Oratory, the church is beautifully gilded and decorated with some excellent works by, among others, **Pietro da Cortona** and Rubens. Neri organized *oratori* (musical get-togethers) here, and the word *oratorio* is now applied to a musical art form, the religious opera, which grew out of these gatherings.

Below: *This impressive trompe l'œil corridor is to be found in the courtyard of Palazzo Spada.*

ancient Rome. Features some fine bronzes, statues and splendid sarcophagi.
- ⊠ *Piazza del Campidoglio*
- ☎ 06 6710-2071
- ⊕ *09:30–20:00 Tue–Sun*

Palazzo Spada

16th-century building renovated by Borromini – he added a marvellous trompe l'œil corridor. The building houses a gallery with both Classical and 17th-century artworks.
- ⊠ *piazza Capo di Ferro 13* ☎ *06 687-4893*
- ⊕ *Closed Monday*
- ♿ €5

Palazzo Altemps

Stunning 15th–16th-century palace set around an elegant courtyard. Contains a wide array of ancient Roman statuary, some collected from the private residence of Julius Caesar.
- ⊠ *via di Sant' Apolinare 44*
- ☎ *06 3996-7700*
- ⊕ *10:00–17:00. Closed Monday* ♿ €5.16

Villa Medici

This beautiful villa has been the site of the French Academy since 1803. It was set up by Louis XIV in 1666.
- ⊠ *Viale Trinità di Monte* ☎ *06 67611*
- ⊕ *Closed Monday.*

Villa Farnesina

Set amid pleasant gardens, the prime attraction at this deep sienna-coloured villa is the stunning ground-floor *Loggia of Cupid and Psyche*, where Raphael painted his sensual frescoes.
- ⊠ *Accademia dei Lincei, via Della Lungara 230*
- ☎ *06 6802-7268*
- ⊕ *09:00–13:00. Closed holidays* ♿ €5

Museums and Galleries

Galleria Nazionale d' Arte Antica

Located in the Piazza Barberini, the most impressive feature is one of Pietro da Cortona's works, the *Triumph of Divine Providence*. Also includes works by a woman thought to be Raphael's mistress.
✉ *palazzo Barberini 18* ☎ *06 482-4184; Information and bookings 06 32810* ⏲ *Closed Monday.*

Capitoline Museums

The Capitoline Museums are housed in Michelangelo's Piazza del Campidoglio and boast one of the finest collections of art, such as ancient Greek and Roman sculptural masterpieces. Among the displays to be seen are bronze and terracotta pieces retrieved from burial chambers north of Rome.
✉ *Piazza del Campidoglio* ☎ *06 6710-2475* ⏲ *09:30–20:00 Tue–Sun*

Museo del Palazzo Venezia

This often-overlooked museum includes some rare ivories from the 8th century, early and mid-Renaissance paintings, ceramics and terracotta models from masters such as Bernini.
✉ *via del Plebiscito 118* ⏲ *09:00–14:00. Closed Monday.*

Museo del Palazzo dei Conservatori

This museum has Classical sculptures and Egyptian and Etruscan items. Also in the building is the Pinacoteca Capitolina, a not-to-be-missed picture gallery with an enviable array of paintings and a valuable collection of porcelain.
✉ *piazza dei Campidoglio 1* ☎ *06 3996-7800* ⏲ *09:00–20:00. Closed Monday.*

Museo Napoleonico

Near the banks of the Tiber, this museum houses a collection most of which came

Above: *A fine Classical carving on rock crystal.*

<u>Unusual Small Museums</u>
Museo Nazionale delle Paste Alimentari (National Museum of Pasta), ✉ piazza Scanderberg 117, ☎ 06 699-1120, 🖥 www.museodellapasta.it All you ever wanted to know about pasta.
Museo Internazionale del Cinema e dello Spettacolo (International Museum of Cinema and Entertainment), ✉ via Portuense 101, ☎ 06 390-0266, 🖥 www.museodelcinema.it Film-making equipment, film library and a vast photographic library.
Piccolo Museo delle Anime del Purgatorio (Museum of the Souls in Purgatory), ✉ Chiesa del Sacro Cuore del Suffragio, Lungotevere Prati 12, ☎ 06 6880-6517. Traces of fire left on cloths, wood tablets and breviaries by souls in Purgatory.

from descendants of the Bonaparte family. It comprises miniatures, jewels and court clothing and was donated by Count Giuseppe Primoli.

✉ *piazza di Ponte Umberto 1,* ☎ *06 6880-6286, 06 687-4240*
🕐 *09:00–19:00. Closed Monday.*

Casa di Goethe

A small museum in the actual rooms in which German poet Goethe stayed. Among the items on display are rare manuscripts, illustrated texts and various first editions.

✉ *via del Corso 18,*
☎ *06 3265-0412*
🕐 *Closed Tuesday.*

Museo di Roma

Housed in the Palazzo Braschi, the museum has a veritable collection of over 40,000 items documenting ordinary life from the Middle Ages to the present. Among the exhibits are ceramics, paintings of historical

events and various sculptures unearthed during demolition and excavation in the 20th century.

✉ *piazza San Pantaleo 10* ☎ *06 8205-9127*
🕐 *09:00–19:30. Closed Monday* ♿ *€6.50*

The Vatican Museums

The Vatican owns an inestimable wealth of visual arts. To see the museums, go early or pre-book timed tickets, otherwise you may queue for hours. Allow at least a full day to do the museums justice. Apart from the Sistine Chapel, the 'must see' museums include: The Raphael Rooms, Pinacoteca (the Vatican Art Gallery), The Etruscan Collection and the Gallery of Modern Religious Art.

✉ *Viale Vaticano, Palazzi Vaticano*
☎ *06 8988-3860*
🕐 *Mar–Oct 08:45–16:45; rest of the year 08:45–13:45. Closed Sunday.*

Castel Sant'Angelo

Conceived by Hadrian as his mausoleum, this castle has been remodelled over the years and has served as a mausoleum for a number of emperors, a papal refuge, garrison for Napoleonic troops and now as a museum. Constructed on four main floors with the papal apartments on the upper storeys.
⊠ On banks of Tiber close to the Vatican
🚌 Bus 40 from Termini station
🕐 09:00–17:00. Closed Monday.

Museo d'Arte Moderna

This museum hosts the best collection of 19th- and 20th-century works in the city. Examples of modern artists include Boccioni, Balla and Severini, as well as other European artists such as Duchamp, Rossetti and van Gogh.
⊠ via Delle Belle Arti 131 ☎ 06 321-714
🕐 Closed Monday.

Museo Nazionale Etrusco

The magnificent collection of Etruscan artefacts from a tomb at Cerveteri (dating back to the 8th century BC) forms this museum. Don't miss the sarcophagus of a noble husband and wife and the collection of drinking cups and vases.
⊠ Piazza Villa Giulia
☎ 06 320-1951
🕐 Open daily.

Museo del Corso

The Museo del Corso is an exhibition space housed in an old palace, offering a variety of temporary art and historic exhibitions.
⊠ via del Corso 320
☎ 06 6389-5746
🕐 Closed Monday.

Appropriate Dress
Visitors to all churches in Italy and any part of the Vatican – including the Gardens and the Museums – are required to dress with appropriate decorum. People wearing short skirts, shorts or tank tops will not be admitted.

More Vatican Museums
Museo Sacro (Museum of early Christian artefacts);
Museo Chiaramonti (Museum of Greek and Roman sculpture);
Museo Gregoriano Profano (Gregorian Museum of Pagan Art and early sculpture).

Opposite: Coronation of the Virgin, by Raphael.
Below: Fresco fragment of an angel by Merlozza da Forli, Pinacoteca, the Vatican.

Parks and Gardens

Giardini Pincio

Beautiful gardens overlooking western Rome. The gardens, with formally laid out avenues of shady trees, statues and fountains, are a favourite place for children, for tourists to admire the panoramic views and for Romans to stroll in the evening.
⊠ *Piazza del Popolo*
M *Flamino/Spagna*

Vatican Gardens

Well worth seeing to gain a different perspective on the Vatican. The well-established trees, well-manicured lawns, grottoes and fountains create a peaceful ambience.
☎ *06 6988-4466*
🕑 *One tour on Mon, Tue, Thu, Sat; not religious holidays*

Orto Botanico

These delightful and well-maintained botanical gardens are not only instructive, but also a pleasure in which to pass a relaxing hour or two. It has a Rose Garden, Japanese Garden, a garden of medicinal herbs and the Monumental Staircase with a 400-year-old plane tree towering over the tiered waterfall.
⊠ *Trastevere*
🕑 *09:30–17:00 winter; 09:30–18:30 summer; closed Sun, Mon, public holidays in Aug.*

Other excellent areas for contact with nature include **Villa Ada**, and various areas of formal gardens, such as the **Giardini Segreti**, the **Viale dell Magnolie** and the **Giardino del Lago**.

Below: *In the midst of the city, the Vatican gardens provide a lush oasis.*

ACTIVITIES
Sport and Recreation

Romans, like Italians in general, adore sport. After all, they hosted the 1960 Olympic Games and the 1990 World Cup. But they prefer to talk about it rather than to swap their designer wear for shirts and shorts. The result is that the precious few facilities that exist in the capital are almost exclusively for members. However, if you are a jogger, you can join the legions in **Villa Borghese** (*see* page 26), the **Pincio Gardens** (*see* page 40) or the **Villa Doria Pamphilj**, many of whom run the dog at the same time. Serious runners can enter the **annual marathon** (late March). For more information, visit ⌨ www.maratona diroma.it/ **Cycling** enthusiasts might want to plan a visit to coincide with the **Giro de Lazio** (June) or the **Giro d'Italia** (May/June) which sometimes passes through Rome. Close to many a Roman heart is the performance of either **Lazio** or **Roma**, the capital's two world-class **soccer** clubs. Games are held most weekends at the **Stadio Olimpico**, ☎ 06 474-4776 for tickets.

> ### Sight Jogging
> If marathons are not high on the priority list, but the need to work off the olive oil-drenched food is still there, a fun way to combine sport and tourism is Sight Jogging. Experienced trainers speaking a variety of different languages become the tour guides and routes and running pace are worked out according to clients' needs.
> It is a great way to see the sights of Rome and keep fit. Plus it is a lot of fun. For more information, visit ⌨ www.sightjogging.it

Below: *Stadio Olimpico during an A.S. Roma match.*

Fun for Children

Most people maintain that Rome is not the ideal place to bring children under the age of seven, because of the loose cobblestones, narrow sidewalks and crowds of people. But with a little bit of planning, nothing can't be done.

Avoid the summer months, opting for either early spring or late autumn. In doing so you will avoid the heat and horrendous crowds. It is also more likely that hotels will be able to arrange a babysitter since they are not as busy as in summer.

Although older children will enjoy the religious and historical sights, there is also a range of fun things to do in and around Rome.

Above: *The parks in the city are a great place for the children to play.*
Opposite: *Gay Village is a ten-week fun-fest.*

Explora Children's Museum

Explora Children's Museum
✉ via Flaminia 82
☎ 06 361-3776
🕒 Visits last 1hr and 45min. 10:00, 12:00, 15:00, 17:00 Tue–Sun and public holidays. Summer time: Jul, Sep 10:00, 12:00, 15:00, 17:00. Aug 12:00 15:00, 17:00. Closed 25 Dec, 1 Jan, 14 Aug, 15 Aug and every Mon.
👶 Children admitted only with an adult. Children under 3 years free, 3–12 years €7; adults €6; groups (min 15) €6.

This child-sized playtown is fun and educational. Through touch, observation and experimentation children can discover the mysteries of everyday life as well as the environment. Booking is essential.

Villa Borghese Gardens

This is a great place to bring children. It is quiet and safe – perfect for a picnic – and offers bumper cars, ponies, family peddle-carts and rowboats for rent. There is also a zoo, a small cinema showing cartoons, and a funfair.

More Fun...

Janiculum Hill: During the summer (every-day, except Wednesday) there are traditional puppet shows.
Villa Celimontana: Has open-air theatre performances during the summer.

Luna Park: On Via della Tre Fontana, this amusement park has fairground rides and a roller coaster. Entrance is free.

Christmas Holiday: If you are in Rome during this time take the children to Piazza Navona for the Befana Christmas Toy Fair. The Nativity at St Peter's Square is also a treat.

Alternative Rome

Although gay and lesbian lifestyles have been conducted more undercover in Rome than in cities like Amsterdam and Cape Town, the past few years have seen more understanding and acceptance amongst heterosexuals for what some of them might perceive as an alternative way of life. In the year 2000, Rome was named the official site of '**World Pride 2000**'. Most recently, in August 2007, Rome's city council officially designated two blocks as a recreational area for gays and lesbians. '**Gay Street**', which stretches from the Colosseum to the Basilica di San Giovanni in Laterno, was introduced to promote culture, fun and solidarity amongst homosexuals.

Gay bars and clubs open up and close down very frequently, so check listings before you go. A popular bar amongst young gays and lesbians is **Coming Out**. It has a relaxed atmosphere, serves cheap drinks and with its view of the Colosseum has a real Italian feel. The best event on the gay calender is undoubtedly **Gay Village**, a ten-week, open-air festival featuring bars, cinemas, restaurants, live acts and dancing. Rome's oldest gay bar, **Hangar**, has a friendly, sexy

Coming Out
✉ via San Giovanni in Laterano 8
☎ 06 700-9871
🕐 17:00–02:00
💰 No credit cards

Gay Village
✉ Parco San Sebastiano, Piazza Numa Pompilio
🖥 www.gayvillage.it
🕐 Late Jun to early Sep 19:00–03:00
💰 No credit cards

Hangar
✉ via in Selci 69A
☎ 06 488-1397
🕐 22:30–02:30 Mon, Wed–Sun. Closed 2 weeks in Aug.
💰 No credit cards

Qube
✉ via di Portonaccio 212 ☎ 06 438-5445
🕐 23:00–05:00 Thu–Sat. Closed mid-Jun–Sep.
💰 €2 Thu; €15 Fri; €8 Sat. No credit cards.

More Information
For general or events information get a copy of the international gay guide *Spartacus*, visit ⌨ www.gay.it/guida/Lazio/Roma (in Italian only) or get a copy of the montly magazine *Pride*. The cultural organization Circolo Mario Mieli di Cultura Omossesuale organizes functions, such as Rome Pride which takes place annually in June. They can be contacted on ☎ 06 541-3958, or visit ⌨ www.mariomieli.it

Classical Rome
Location: Map C

Start: San Clemente Papa al Laterano

Finish: Roman Forum or Circo Massimo

Below: *The three remaining columns of the temple of Castor and Pollux, Roman Forum.*

atmosphere and is packed on weekends and on 'Striptease Thursday'. Another bar to check out is **Qube**, one of Rome's biggest clubs. It features live rock shows on Thursdays, while the Muccassassina drag queens offer light-hearted entertainment on Fridays. For more details *see* panel, page 43.

For something a bit different, make use of Rome's only gay-owned limousine sightseeing service. The company offers a gay night out special as well as gay concierge services. For more information, visit ⌨ www.gaylimorome.com

Walking Tours
The best way to see Rome is on foot. It is obviously more tiring than taking a bus or taxi trip, but it is also more rewarding. Don't be afraid to get lost in the small side streets; some of the more worthwhile, less commercial sights are a little off the beaten track. Just be aware of pickpockets and beggars.

Classical Rome
Start at **San Clemente Papa al Laterano** and walk west down Via di San Giovanni in Laterano. Continue until the end of the road, at which point the **Colosseum** will be in front of you. The entrance is to your right – continue around the Colosseum into Piazza del Colosseo. Walking south from here you will see the **Arch of Constantine**. Walk north over the piazza and turn left into Via dei Fori Imperiali. Continue down the road, then

turn left into Via Tulliano, then turn left again into Via Salara Vecchia. This road leads to the **Roman Forum**. Walking south over the Forum leads you to **Palatine Hill**. If there is more time, walk back over the Forum the same way as you came

and back into Via dei Fori Imperiali. Walk northwest down the road, around the bend and **Piazza Venezia** will be on the right. Continue with the road and it becomes Via del Teatro di Marcello. Continue south into Via Petroselli, into **Piazza Bocca della Verità**. **Santa Maria in Cosmedin** is located here. At the church turn right into Via dei Ara Massima di Ercole, then turn left into Via del Circo Massimo. Continue with the road and you will see **Circo Massimo** on the left.

Above: *Quiet corners around the Fontana di Trevi are filled with cafés, ideal for a quick reviver.*

Baroque Rome
Location: Map D

Start: Piazza del Popolo

Finish: Fontana di Trevi

Baroque Rome

Start at **Piazza del Popolo**. Walking south you wil see two churches, **Santa Maria dei Miracoli** and **Santa Maria in Montesanto**. Continue walking straight down, walking along Via del Babuino. This road leads to **Piazza di Spagna**. Continue south over the piazza to Piazza Mignanelli. From there turn left and walk towards **Via Sistina**. Walk southeast down the road, cross Via Francesco Crispi, and continue. Then turn left into Via Barberini, where **Palazzo Barberini** is located. Walk back down Via Barberini and continue west into Via del Tritone. Walk across Via del Traforo and take the second left, which will lead to **Fontana di Trevi**.

Tour Tips
The best buy in Rome, if you are into history and the arts, is the **Roma Pass**. In a 3-day period, this bundle of offers enables the holder two free museum entrances, reduced costs for all participating museums and sites and free transport on Rome's bus and metro system. It is available from the tourist offices and participating museums. Currently it costs €20 per pass.

Above: *The interior of the Pantheon incorporates architecture from many different eras.*

Tickets
The **Archeologica Card**, available from participating sights and museums, is a €22, 7-day pass to many of the top archaeological sights and museums, including the Colosseum.
The **Go Card** (🖳 www.gocard.org) is a 1-year card for those aged 14–26, offering hefty discounts to many sights, shops, bars and cinemas. 🖳 www. weekendaroma.com actually charges a premium, but you can prebook timed tickets to popular sights and save yourself several hours in a queue.

Piazza Navona to Palazzo Doria Pamphilj
Start at **Piazza Navona** and walk north over the square to Via Zanardelli. Turn right then turn left in Piazza Sant' Apollinare. Walk north over the piazza, turn right and walk towards the church of **San Agostino**. Walk southeast across Piazza San Agostino to Via della Scrofa. Walk south (right) towards **Piazza San Luigi dei Francesi** where the church of the same name is located. From the church walk east down Via Giustiniani towards the **Piazza Rotunda**, which is where the **Pantheon** is. Walk south to Piazza Minerva and **Santa Maria sopra Minerva** will be on the left. From the church walk left down Via S. C. da Siena then right into Via del Gesù. Continue down the road then turn left into Via del Plebiscito. Walk down the road, Palazzo Altieri will be on the left and the church Chiesa del Gesù on the right. Continue along Via del Plebiscito until you see **Palazzo Doria Pamphilj** on your left.

Jewish Rome to Trastevere

From **Teatro di Marcello** in Piazza Monte Savello walk north into **Via Portico d'Ottavia**. On the corner of this road and Via Catalana is the **Synagogue**. Continue in a northwesterly direction along Via Portico d'Ottavia. At the end of this street is **Sant'Angelo in Pescheria**. Turn left into **Via Arenula** and continue south down the road then cross the Ponte Garibaldi into **Trastevere**. Turn right into Lung. d. Farnesina, walk straight, then turn left into Via Giuseppe Garibaldi. Turn left into Via d. Scala, and continue down the road into **Piazza Santa Maria in Trastevere**, where the **church** is located. From here walk back into Via d. Scala and head northwest into Via della Lungara. Walk down the road and you will see **Palazzo Corsini** on your left and **Villa Farnesina** on your right.

Two Churches and a Market

Start at **Piazza Santa Maria Maggiore** (the **church** of the same name is located here). Walk south down Via Merulana. Continue straight into **Piazza San Gionvanni in Laterano**, where the cathedral of the Diocese of Rome is located. From the church walk southeast to Piazza Porta San Giovanni. The Via Sannio market, one of the most popular markets in Rome, is located to the south.

Below: *The Basilica di San Giovanni in Laterano.*

Bus Tours

110
☎ 06 4695-2252
🕐 Departs every 15min,
Oct–Mar 09:00–20:00;
Apr–Sep 09:00–20:30

Citysightseeing Roma
☎ 06 228-3957
🖥 www.
roma.city-sightseeing.it

Ciao Roma
🕐 Departs 10:00, 11:00,
12:00, 14:00, 15:00
from the Stazione
Termini.

Green Line
☎ 06 482-7480
🖥 www.
greenlinetours.com
📧 booking@
greenlinetours.com

Rome Open Tour
☎ 06 8530-1758
🕐 Departs every 25min

Organized Tours
Bus Tours
There are lots of 'hop-on, hop-off' bus tours that go by the main sights in Rome and offer commentaries as they travel. They are all around €15 and usually leave from Piazza Cinquecento (in front of **Stazione Termini**) before passing by some 10–12 different stops. You can board or leave as you wish. If the weather is great, start early as they get overly crowded and you may not have a seat. The companies to look out for include **110**, **Citysightseeing Roma**, **Ciao Roma**, **Green Line** or **Rome Open Tour**. The **Archeobus** (€8) is a similar hop-on, hop-off bus that leaves from Platform E of the Stazione Termini and travels via a number of archaeological sites to Via Appia Antica and other more far-flung parts of Rome where you'll find more archaeological sites. There are also **Rome by Night** and **Basilica Tours** in season. Information and tickets from the **ATAC** information booth in front of Termini Station, ☎ 06 4695-4695.

Bike or Hike
Bici & Baci rents out bikes, scooters and motorbikes – including insurance and hel-

Right: *Driving around on a scooter is a wonderful way to see the sights.*

Left: A number of tour companies offer guided boat cruises along the River Tiber.

mets in the price. **Enjoy Rome** offers – amongst a host of services – guided walking tours around various areas of Rome, and also guided bike tours. **Landimension Travel** also runs guided city tours by electric bike.

Boat Trips

Battelli di Roma offers guided cruises along the Tiber from Ponte San Angelo.

Tourvisa Italia operates 100-minute mini-cruises (board beneath Ponte Umberto I on the Lungotevere Tor di Nona) to and from Ponte Duca d'Aosta.

Walking Tours

Roma Antica runs fascinating walking tours with highly qualified guides. **Walking Tours Rome** offers day- and night-time guided walks with commentary in English.

Bioparco di Roma

Villa Borghese, ⊠ Ple del Giardino Zoologico 1, ☎ 06 360-8211, 🖳 www.bioparco.it This attractive zoo, at the top of the Villa Borghese park, is fun for those who may need a break from Rome's history (*see also* Fun For Kids, page 42).

Bike or Hike
Bici & Baci
⊠ via del Viminale 5
☎ 06 482-8443
🖳 www.bicibaci.com

Enjoy Rome
⊠ via Marghera 8
☎ 06 445-1843
🖳 www.enjoyrome.com

Landimension Travel
⊠ via Ostilia 10
☎ 06 7759-1009
🖳 www.
landimensiontravel.it

Boat Trips
Battelli di Roma
⊠ via della Tribuna Tor
de' Spechi 15
☎ 06 9774-5414 or
0678-9361
🖳 www.
battellidiroma.it

Tourvisa Italia
☎ 06 448-741
🖳 www.
tourvisaitalia.com

Walking Tours
Roma Antica
☎ 06 4544-3179
🖳 www.
roma-antica.co.uk

Walking Tours Rome
☎ 06 2329-6896
🖰 Info@
walkingrome.com
🖳 www.
walkingrome.com

Right: *Piazza Navona is a good place to buy original watercolours of Rome and the Roman countryside.*

Department Stores

Rome is not well endowed with department stores, preferring small retailers and boutiques. For a selection of clothing and household items, head for the following department stores:

La Rinascente, ✉ via del Corso 189 (fairly up-market) or Plaza Sta Maria Maggiore; **Upim**, ✉ via del Tritone 172 or via Giolitti 10 (Staz. Termini); **Oviesse**, ✉ via Piazza V. Emanuele 108 (Vatican) or viale Trastevere 62; the shopping centre at **Cinecittà Due (M** Subaugusta) is also a good hunting ground. Lastly, **Discount dell' Alta Moda**, ✉ via Gesù e Maria 14–16 (near Piazza Popolo), is the place for Italian high-fashion bargains.

Shops

The places to shop for designer fashion goods such as shoes and clothes are **Via Condotti** and **Via Borgognona** (*see page 29*). But the side streets between them are also good shopping streets. You'll find young fashions, leather, shoes, jewellery, art, antiques, porcelain, cutlery, handmade paper and linen.

Dress Agency Donna

This second-hand shop dealing in designer-wear is a good option for those who don't want to spend a fortune on fashion, but would like something unique.

✉ *via del Vantaggio 1/B near Piazza del Popolo,*
☎ *06 321-0898*

Bonora

If time permits treat yourself to a pair of handmade shoes. For over 120 years Bonora has offered both ready-made and handcrafted men's shoes.

✉ *via del Babuino 32,*
☎ *06 3600-6909,*
⊕ *09:00–19:30 daily*

Petrocchi

Another store offering handmade and ready-made shoes. Count on a minimum of $700 and allow 2–3 weeks for the manufacture of the shoes.

✉ *via dell'Orso 25,*
☎ *06 687-6289,*
⊕ *09:00–19:30 daily*

Bookshops

Want a good read or some background material on Ancient Rome? The following bookshops have new and second-hand books in English. **Feltrinelli,** ✉ via VE Orlando 84 (**M** Repubblica) or via del Babuino 39/40; **Anglo-American Book Co.,** ✉ via delle Vite 102, Tridente 🖳 www.aab.it; **Mel Bookstore,** ✉ via Nazionale 254 (**M** Repubblica); **The English Bookshop,** ✉ via di Ripetta 248 (**M** Flaminio); **The Lion Bookshop,** ✉ via dei Greci 33 (**M** Spagna); **Bibli,** ✉ via dei Fienaroli (☎ 06 581-4534).

Antiques

The narrow streets filtering into old Rome on the western side of **Piazza Navona** form a neighbourhood little frequented by visitors. There are, however, a wealth of small, local shops and antique dealers. Pedestrian-only **Via Coronari** is the scene of Rome's annual antiques fair.

Good Reading

Barrett, Anthony, *Agrippina*, Routledge, 1996. Historical.

David, Elizabeth, *Italian Food*, Penguin, 1998. Cookery book from the English-language doyenne of European cuisine.

Gibbon, Edward, *The Decline and Fall of the Roman Empire*, Penguin, 1982. Historical literature.

Graves, Robert and **Francis, Richard**, *I Claudius*, Carcanet Press, 1998. Accurately documented fiction in Ancient Rome.

Hare, Augustus, *Augustus Hare in Italy*, Michael Russell Publications, 1977 (19th century text, re-published).

McCullough, Colleen, *The First Man in Rome*, Arrow, 1992; *Caesar's Women*, Arrow, 1997. Finely researched fiction set in Ancient Rome.

Moravia, Alberto, *The Conformist*, Prion, 1999. Contemporary fiction, translated.

Saylor, Steven, *The House of the Vestals*, Robinson Publishing, 1999. Accurately documented fiction set in Ancient Rome.

Stone, Irving, *The Agony and the Ecstasy*. Mandarin, 1989. Novel based on facts about Michelangelo.

Yallop, David, *In God's Name*, Corgi, 1997. Finely researched novel about papal intrigue.

Bargaining

Prices are fixed in stores, but you can try bargaining when shopping in the markets.

Most importantly, when buying goods from street vendors, do not accept their initial price. Go into a fixed-price store and find out their price, then look at the price at other street stalls. Here you can bargain to your heart's content. If you do not like the final price, walk away. You are guaranteed to find the same article (probably for much less) a few metres down the street.

Below: *Merchandise of all sorts and authenticity finds its way to the Porta Portese Sunday Market.*

Markets
Porta Portese Sunday Market

Each Sunday morning a sprawling flea market unfolds along Via Portuense and Via Hippolito Nievo around Porta Portese, the 17th-century city gate that was built by Urban VIII. Merchandise such as books, second-hand clothes, bric-a-brac, household gadgets, spices and wholesome foods, furniture, antiques and items of dubious origin are sold to keen browsers and other dealers. It is colourful and full of character.

✉ *Piazza di Porta Portese*
M *Tram 8 from Torre Argentina*
🕐 *05:00–13:00 Sunday*

Via Sannio Street Market

Just beyond the city walls, a five-minute walk from San Giovanni in Laterano, lies one of the city's most popular markets. This is one of the best places in Rome for clothes and shoes (new, bargain and second-hand), leather goods, books, kitchen knick-knacks, CDs and souvenirs. The semi-covered area at the far end of the market is the most useful area for finding bargain seconds and military-style clothing.

✉ *Via Sannio*
M *San Giovanni*
🕐 *08:30–13:00 Mon–Sat.*

Mercato di Piazza Vittorio Emanuele

Ginger, mangoes, soya, dried fish and pungent chillies do not readily spring to mind when you think of Italian markets, but the large street market around picturesque Piazza V.

Emanuele is the focal point for African and Asian ingredients. Fresh or dried. Italian fruit and vegetables feature also. Get there early for the best buys – and watch your bags in the crowds.

☒ *Piazza Vittorio Emanuele*
M *Vittorio Emanuele*
⏰ *07:00–14:00 Mon–Sat*

Mercantino dei Partigiani

Small, inexpensive flea market in the basement of a garage. Sells mostly objects from the 40s and 50s.

☒ *Piazza dei Partigiani*
⏰ *1st Sun of the month, except Aug.*

Underground

Relatively new flea market in a large four-floor garage between Piazza del Popolo and Via Veneto. Has a bit of everything, but prices are on the high side.

☒ *Via Crispi 96*

M *Hospital Clinic*
⏰ *2nd Sat and Sun of the month.*

Olympic Village Market

Typical country market selling food, clothing and jewellery. Excellent prices.

☒ *Viale della XVII Olimpiade*
⏰ *Friday only.*

Little Market of Borgo Parioli

Weekly market selling antiques, books, furniture and jewellery.

☒ *via Tirso 14 to via Metauro 21*
⏰ *10:00–20:00 Sat and Sun. Closed last Sun of the month.*

Above: *The fragrant flower stalls in the Mercato di Piazza Vittorio Emanuele.*

Buying Food at a Supermarket

Although buying food at a local supermarket is not much different in Rome, there are a few differences. Some large supermarkets might charge you €1 for the use of a shopping cart, so have the money handy as you need it to free the cart. When selecting fruit and vegetables you need to wear plastic gloves (supplied). It is also expected of you to weigh your bag of fruit or vegetables yourself and put the price sticker on the bag. When paying you might have to pay for a carrier bag and you always have to bag the groceries yourself.

Above: *The Bernini Bristol hotel has an amazing rooftop view of Rome.*

Accommodation Tips
It is not easy to find quality, inexpensive accommodation. As the high season runs for eight months, rooms are always in demand. It is therefore important to reserve before arriving. Popular areas to find a hotel include Piazza di Spagna, Campo de' Fiori, Via Cavour and the Termini area around the station. Most of Rome's sights and a wealth of restaurants are either walking distance or accessible by bus from these areas. However, for something less expensive, think of the area around the Colosseum, the north side of Stazione Termini and some of the hotels in Borgo, near the Vatican. Travel time is a little more but that is compensated by some less expensive prices.

WHERE TO STAY

Hotel accommodation in central Rome is among the most costly in Europe, and you pay for the privilege of living in a historic building or ancient neighbourhood. Modestly priced rooms are hard to find, although room rates can be negotiated out of high season (Apr–Oct inclusive, Easter and Christmas). Many historic neighbourhoods – such as Campo de' Fiori, Piazza Navona and Piazza di Spagna – do not allow cars without local permits to enter. Parking is non-existent, and the best solution is to arrive by taxi or on foot. If you are visiting Rome by car, *see* page 86 for where to leave your car and use public transport.

In the following listings, a double room in the high season is classified as follows: **Budget** €60–125 (at the lower prices, bathrooms are sometimes shared); **Mid-range** €125–200 (these include private facilities); **Luxury** €200–300. Those well over €250 (and there are quite a large number) are classified as **De Luxe**. If you arrive without a hotel, a useful service for a few Euro per reservation is the hotel reservation system at Stazione Termini (☎ 06 699-1000, 🖥 www.hotelreservation.it) which offers up-to-the-minute information on availability before making a reservation.

Bed and breakfast is a growing industry in Rome, offering excellent, often extremely reasonable accommodation. The APT (*see* page 84) publishes a list of establishments, while 🖥 www.flatinrome.com offers a range of self-catering apartments.

• DE LUXE
Hotel de Russie
(Map D–D2)
Stylishly modern boutique hotel; charming garden restaurant and bar and a sybaritic, full-service spa; a few minutes' walk from the Spanish Steps.
✉ via del Babuino 9,
☎ 06 328-881,
🖷 06 3288-8888,
💻 www.hotelderussie.com

Westin Excelsior
(Map D–F3)
Sumptuously renovated historic hotel with one of the city's finest addresses, gilded décor and a guest list to match.
✉ via Vittorio Veneto 125, ☎ 06 4708-7911,
🖷 06 482-6205,
💻 www.starwoodhotels.com/westin/

Hotel Hassler Villa Medici (Map D–E3)
Historic, privately owned five-star hotel with an international reputation and superb location.
✉ piazza Trinità dei Monti 6,
☎ 06 69-9340,
🖷 06 678-9991,
💻 www.hotelhasslerroma.com

Raphael (Map D–C4)
Brightly, sometimes unusually, but always charmingly decorated four-star hotel in a tiny piazza.
✉ largo Febo 2,
☎ 06 68-2831,
🖷 06 687-8993,
💻 www.raphaelhotel.com

Sheraton Roma Hotel (Map E–C4)
Large, comfortable four-star hotel with gym and outdoor pool in the EUR business district.
✉ viale del Pattinaggio 100,
☎ 06 54-531,
🖷 06 594-0689,
💻 www.starwoodhotels.com/sheraton

Boscolo Hotel Exedra (Map D–G4)
Ultra-chic, ultra-modern five-star hotel in the heart of Rome, with spa, garden and roof terrace.
✉ piazza della Repubblica 47,
☎ 06 489-381,
🖷 06 4893-8000,
💻 www.exedra.boscolohotels.com

Le Grand Hotel
(Map D–G4)
The first de luxe hotel in Rome. Built in 1894, this 161-room hotel is within walking distance of major tourist attractions such as the Spanish Steps and Via Veneto. Reputed to be one of the best hotels in the world.
✉ via Vittorio Emanuele Orlando 3,
☎ 06 647-091,
🖷 06 474-7307,
💻 www.stregis.com

Bernini Bristol
(Map D–F3)
This luxury 127-room hotel is centrally located in the heart of Rome. It has banqueting rooms, fitness club, and a rooftop restaurant with an amazing view.
✉ piazza Barberini 23,
☎ 06 488-3051,
🖷 06 482-4266,
💻 www.sinahotels.it

• *LUXURY*

Hotel Massimo d'Azeglio

(Map D–G4)

For over 130 years, smart hotel in the classic style. Near Sta Maria Maggiore and Termini.

✉ *via Cavour 18,*
☎ *06 464-0561,*
🖳 *www.*
romehoteldazeglio.it

Hotel Gladiatori

(Map C–D1)

Charming small hotel in a renovated hunting lodge overlooking the Colosseum. Rooftop terrace.

✉ *via Labicana 125,*
☎ *06 7759-1380,*
📠 *06 7005-638,*
🖳 *www.*
hotelgladiatori.it

Hotel Celio

(Map C–D2)

Small three-star hotel just behind the Colosseum, delightfully decorated in Renaissance themes.

✉ *via dei Santi Quattro 35/C,* ☎ *06 7049-5333,*
📠 *06 709-6377,*
🖳 *www.*
hotelcelio.com

Hotel Forum

(Map D–E6)

Four-star hotel with great location and good service. Fine views from rooftop restaurant.

✉ *via Tor de' Conti 25–30,* ☎ *06 679-2446,*
📠 *06 678-6479,*
🖳 *www.*
hotelforumrome.com

Hotel Condotti

(Map D–D3)

Attractive small three-star hotel with appealing rooms and good facilities.

✉ *via Mario de' Fiori 37,* ☎ *06 679-4661,*
📠 *06 679-0457,*
🖳 *www.*
hotelcondotti.com

Hotel Manfredi

(Map D–D2)

Small exclusive three-star hotel, decorated with antiques.

✉ *via Margutta 61,*
☎ *06 320-7676,*
📠 *06 320-7736,*
🖳 *www.hmanfredi.com*

Hotel Locarno

(Map D–C2)

Old-world, three-star hotel, conveniently located near Piazza del Popolo (one of Rome's largest cobblestone squares).

✉ *via della Penna 22,*
☎ *06 361-0841,*
📠 *06 321-5249,*
🖳 *www.*
hotellocarno.com

Hotel Columbus

(Map D–A4)

Former palace of princes and cardinals, now a chic four-star hotel.

✉ *via della Conciliazione 33,*
☎ *06 686-5435,*
📠 *06 686-4874,*
🖳 *www.*
hotelcolumbus.net

Hotel Atlante Star

(Map D–A3)

Very comfortable four-star hotel with rooftop restaurant and terrace for great views of St Peter's.

✉ *via Vitelleschi 34,*
☎ *06 687-3233,*
📠 *06 687-2300,*
🖳 *www.*
atlantehotels.com

Hotel Villa Borghese (Map D–F1)

Mid-sized, family-run,

slightly old-fashioned three-star hotel with good service.

✉ via Pinciana 31,
☎ 06 8530-0919,
✆ 06 841-4100,
💻 www.
hotelvillaborghese.it

Hotel Atlantico

(Map D–G4)
Four-star hotel located on the highest of Rome's seven hills. It has modern, comfortable rooms and is within walking distance of the Trevi Fountain and the Colosseum.

✉ via Cavour 23,
☎ 06 485-951,
✆ 06 482-7492,
💻 www.
bettojahotels.it

Imperiale Hotel

(Map D–E3)
Recently refurbished 95-room hotel close to some of the 'must see' tourist attractions.

✉ via Vittorio Veneto 24,
☎ 06 482-6351,
✆ 06 474-2583,
💻 www.
hotelimperialeroma.it

• MID-RANGE

Hotel Teatro di Pompeo (Map D–C5)

Unusual three-star hotel, built on the remains of an ancient Roman theatre. Simple, comfortable interiors.

✉ largo del Pallaro 8,
☎ 06 6830-0170,
✆ 06 6880-5531,
💻 www.hotelteatro dipompeo.it
📧 hotel.teatrodi pompeo@tiscalinet.it

Hotel Nord Nuova Roma (Map D–G4)

This well-situated, modernized hotel has a pretty rooftop terrace.

✉ via Amendola 3,
☎ 06 488-5441,
💻 www.
romehotelnord.it

Hotel Campo de' Fiori (Map D–C5)

Pretty vine-clad two-star hotel in heart of pedestrian-only, old Rome.

✉ via del Biscione 6,
☎ 06 6880-6865,
✆ 06 687-6003,
💻 www.
hotelcampodefiori.com

Hotel Mozart

(Map D–D3)
Delightful three-star hotel, small but smart, in excellent location.

✉ via del Greci 23/B,
☎ 06 3600-1915,
✆ 06 3600-1735,
💻 www.
hotelmozart.com

Hotel Forte

(Map D–D3)
Small, smart three-star hotel in excellent location.

✉ via Margutta 61,
☎ 06 320-7625,
✆ 06 320-2707,
💻 www.
hotelforte.com
📧 orte@italyhotel.com

Hotel Piazza di Spagna (Map D–D3)

In the heart of Rome, pretty, charmingly furnished vine-clad three-star hotel.

✉ via Mario de' Fiori 61, ☎ 06 679-3061,
✆ 06 679-0654,
💻 www.
hotelpiazzadispagna.it

Hotel Alimandi

(Map A–B1)
Three-star hotel near Vatican Museums.

✉ via Tunisi 8,
☎ 06 3972-3948,
📠 06 3972-3941,
💻 www.alimandi.it

Hotel Sant' Anna

(Map A–C2)
Just off St Peter's
Square, finely furn-
ished 16th-century
three-star pension.
✉ Borgo Pio 134,
☎ 06 6880-1602,
📠 06 6830-8717,
💻 www.
hotelsantanna.com

Hotel Marghera

(Map D–H4)
This simple and com-
fortable three-star
hotel is near Termini
station.
✉ via Marghera 29,
☎ 06 445-7184,
📠 06 446-2539,
💻 www.
hotelmarghera.it

Hotel Borromeo

(Map D–G5)
Smart three-star hotel
in renovated building;
good location.
✉ via Cavour 117,
☎ 06 48-5856,
📠 06 488-2541,
💻 www.
hotelborromeo.com

Hotel Bramante

(Map D–A4)
Beautifully decorated
16th-century inn near
the Vatican. Sixteen
rooms and some
apartments.
✉ vicolo delle Palline
24, ☎ 06 6880-6426,
📠 06 6813-3339,
💻 www.
hotelbramante.com

Hotel Lancelot

(Map C–D2)
Attractive little hotel
a quick walk from the
Colosseum.
✉ via Capo D'Africa
47, ☎ 06 7045-0615,
📠 06 7045-0640,
💻 www.
lancelothotel.com

Abruzzi Hotel

(Map D–D4)
Comfortable three-
star hotel in the
heart of Rome. Faces
the Pantheon and is
withing walking dis-
tance of the Spanish
Steps.
✉ piazza della
Rotonda 69,
☎ 06 679-2021,
📠 06 6978-8076,
💻 www.
hotelabruzzi.it

Kennedy Hotel

(Map D–H5)
Founded in 1963 to
honour the memory
of American president
John F. Kennedy, this
three-star hotel is
open 24 hours and is
close to the Termini
station.
✉ via Filippo Turati
62-64, ☎ 06 446-5373,
📠 06 446-5417,
💻 www.
hotelkennedy.net

Gregoriana Hotel

(Map D–E3)
Art Deco hotel locat-
ed near the Piazza di
Spagna. Simple, but
spacious rooms and
bathrooms and first
class service. Was pre-
viously a convent.
✉ via Gregoriana 18,
☎ 06 679-4269,
📠 06 678-4258.

• BUDGET

Perugia (Map C–C1)
Small but pleasant
one-star hotel in quiet
street in the centre of
town.
✉ via del Colosseo 7,
☎ 06 679-7200,
📠 06 678-4635,
💻 www.hperugia.it

Hotel Navona
(Map D–C5)
Recently renovated one-star hotel in an old palazzo, built on the site of Agrippa's Baths.
✉ via dei Sediari 8,
☎ 06 686-4203,
✆ 06 6880-3802,
💻 www.hotelnavona.com

Hotel Panda
(Map D–D3)
Excellent location, simple two-star pension. Surrounded by excellent restaurants and fashion boutiques.
✉ via della Croce 35,
☎ 06 678-0179,
✆ 06 6994-2151,
💻 www.hotelpanda.it

Residence Candia
(Map A–B1)
Small and medium-sized apartments, located just five minutes from the Vatican Museums.
✉ via Candia 135B,
☎/✆ 06 3972-1046,
💻 www.residencecandia.it
✉ residence.candia@srd.it

Hotel Adriatic
(Map D–A3)
Near the Vatican; decent two-star hotel with good-sized rooms.
✉ via Giovanni Vitelleschi 25,
☎ 06 6880-8080,
✆ 06 689-3552,
💻 www.adriatichotel.com

Pensione Dino
(Map D–H4)
Small, friendly one-star pension; on the better side of Termini station in a bustling neighbourhood. Private rooms are also available.
✉ via Milazzo 14, 1st floor, ☎ 06 4470-2456, ✆ 06 495-7243,
💻 www.hoteldino.net
✉ hoteldino@hotmail.com

Ferraro Hotel
(Map D–F6)
Small, clean and well-run one-star hotel. Walking distance from the Colosseum.
✉ via Cavour 266, 2nd floor, ☎ 06 4890-6292,
✆ 06 474-3683,
💻 www.hotelferraro.it

Hotel Paba
(Map D–F6)
Intimate and homely hotel near the Colosseum and the Roman Forum.
✉ via Cavour 266, 2nd floor,
☎ 06 4782-4902,
✆ 06 4788-1225,
💻 www.hotelpaba.com

Pomezia Hotel
(Map D–C5)
Quiet and comfortable two-star hotel surrounded by good restaurants. Located between Campo de' Fiori and Piazza Navona. Rooms have private toilet and shower.
✉ via dei Chiavari 12,
☎ 06 686-1371,
✆ 06 686-1371.

Prati Hotel
(Map D–A3)
Small, quiet two-star hotel with friendly service. Centrally located.
✉ via Crescenzio 89,
☎ 06 687-5357,
✆ 06 6880-6938,
💻 www.hotelprati-roma.com

Italian *Gelati*

Savouring scoops of Italian ice cream in a cone or tub is one of the pleasures of strolling the Roman streets in summer. The finest *gelati* are the home-made ones. The tradition of making ices goes back to the 17th century and it has even been suggested that the idea originated in **China** and was brought to Italy by **Marco Polo**. The best ice creams, which are often water and fruit ices, are from **Giolitti** (✉ Via degli Uffici del Vacario), **Tre Scalini** (✉ piazza Navona 28), **Caffé ai Tre Tarfufi** (✉ piazza Navona 27), **Palazzo del Freddo** (✉ Via Principe Eugenio, behind Piazza V. Emanuele) and **La Fonte della Salute** (✉ via Marmaggi Cardinale 2, Trastevere).

Below: *An open-air trattoria.*

EATING OUT
Food and Drink

Rome is not the culinary capital of Italy, but Romans certainly give cuisine its due importance. While breakfasts are rarely more than a strong *caffè* or frothy cappuccino and a feather-light flaky pastry in a convenient bar on the way to work, the *aperitivo*, lunch and dinner take on some importance. From April to the end of October, most restaurants with outdoor space will open their terraces or pavement seating, crowding tables and large umbrellas into their allotted space. It is usually a squeeze but this is part of the charm of dining alfresco.

Where to Eat

The tourist in Rome will find a bewildering variety of names for places to eat: each has its merits. At the bottom of the eateries is the humble *osteria*, an inexpensive hostelry, originally a place to stop for a meal or drink on a journey. Today's *osteria* might be nearer a wine bar in atmosphere, or it may offer a rustic atmosphere with good home cooking and fair prices. Slightly more up-market, the *trattoria* is a homely place (often entirely run by one family) with local cuisine. Some of Rome's best-loved *trattorie* are far from simple affairs and the prices

reflect the quality of cuisine and a well-heeled clientele. An *enoteca*, another popular alternative, is the equivalent of a wine bar, complete with a fine selection of wines and snacks. If you want a quick bite without formality, a *tavola calda* is the answer. This delicatessen-type eatery offers an array of ready-made dishes, usually sold by weight, which will be heated for you and can either

Above: Gelatarias *are common in Rome and a relief in the hot summer months.*

be eaten on the premises or taken away. The ubiquitous *pizzeria* often serves more than just pizzas but the best invariably come from a genuine *pizzeria* – wood fire, home-made dough and real mozzarella cheese. Alternatively, pre-cooked pizza slices are a great and economic snack for busy sightseers.

For a full meal, head for a *ristorante*; a *trattoria ristorante* will produce various local dishes, while a *ristorante* denotes a smarter locale with, perhaps, non-local dishes and pretensions to grandeur. Naturally, this also costs a bit more.

Rome is not a cheap place to eat. The only way to eat inexpensively is to buy food in the local supermarkets, or to stick to fast food such as pizza. Expect to pay at least €30 for a two-course lunch or dinner

Eating Out Tips
Most restaurants post a menu at the entrance, so check out specialities and prices before entering as bills are often much more than anticipated. Cover charge is always added to an à la carte meal. A service charge is sometimes included and government taxes (IVA, similar to VAT) are sometimes itemized as extras on the bill. Look for restaurants and cafés well patronized by Italians.

Above: *Bread, breadsticks and rolls are usually served with meals.*

Rome's Oldest Restaurant
Dating back to 1528, **La Campana**, ✉ vicolo della Campana 18, ☎ 06 686-7820, is the city's oldest and one of its favourite dining spots. Celebrated guests who have feasted here on its traditional *cucina Romana* include **Goethe**, **Picasso** and **Pasolini**. Dishes to sample include its *abacchio al forno* (roast lamb) and *cervello ai carciofi* (brains in artichokes). The artichoke *ravioli* are also superb, as are the courgette (squash/zucchini) flowers stuffed with anchovies and mozzarella. Fish dishes are also very popular.

with wine and mineral water, and more for a more elaborate multi-course meal with wine. Budget restaurants generally cost less than €25 per person. A meal in a mid-range restaurant should be between €30 and €60 while a meal costing more than this is categorized as luxury. Most restaurants close one day a week, usually Sunday or Monday. Phone to check. In peak season, eat early or make a reservation. The most popular areas for restaurants are Campo de' Fiori, Piazza Navona, Piazza di Spagna, Trastevere and the Ghetto. For more information, try: 🖳 www.ristorantidiroma.com

On the Menu

Roman restaurants are particularly good with *antipasti*. These cold dishes, varying from cooked vegetables to Parma ham, salamis and seafood, are presented on a trolley and are designed to whet the appetite before the *pasto*, or main meal, arrives.

Pasta – sometimes coloured green, orange or mulberry and served with an imaginative range of sauces (*see* panel, this page) – usually constitutes the *primo piatto*, or first dish. **Rice**, too, is a favourite starter. *Risotto* (savoury rice dishes) include *risotto alla Romana*, with sweetbreads, liver and topped with slivers of cheese. *Bruschetta* are slices of bread rubbed with garlic and topped with chopped tomatoes and basil, which also make a good starter. Bread is always provided with a meal, but you pay for it – sometimes for each roll!

Secondi piatti, or **main courses**, to look out for are *abacchio*, tender roast lamb prepared in the oven and which, when well cooked, falls off the bone; *vitello* (veal), which is offered as a scallop; a mouthwatering dish that includes Parma ham (known as *saltimbocca*), or is made with Marsala and sage. *Bifstecca* (steak) is usually cut fairly thin and grilled quickly to seal in the flavour. *Pollo* (chicken) will invariably feature on the menu: *Petto di Pollo* (chicken breast) is a popular and inexpensive dish, while *Pollo al Diavolo* (chicken in tomato and capsicum peppers) is often an excellent choice. Offal generally has less success with tourists than locals. Sweetbreads, *fegato* (liver) and *coda* (oxtail) are on most menus. There is plenty of fresh *pesce* (fish) available in Rome, but it is often the most expensive item on a menu. Usually grilled, the most popular include *rombo* (turbot), *baccalà* (cod), *spigola* (sea bass) and *sogliola* (sole). *Fritto misto* (mixed fried fish) can be delicious.

Garibaldi Biscuits

A type of biscuit containing a layer of currants was favoured by the Italian patriot Garibaldi, and named after him. Popular theory asserts that the currants represent the flies found in his rations when on campaign.

Pasta

Durum wheat flour, water and sometimes eggs make up most pasta, occasionally coloured with spinach or tomato. It comes in all shapes, laced with a myriad sauces and served *al dente*. Romans love **tagliatelle** and **fettuccine** (both ribbon noodles), **penne** (quills), **farfalle** (butterfly-shaped bites) and **fusilli** (spirals). Pasta parcels filled with cheese or meats are presented as **tortellini** or **ravioli**. Try, also, **gnocchi** (small cocoons made from potato flour). Favourite sauces include melted cheeses, **fior di zucchini** (courgette flowers), **pesto**, **carbonara** (eggs, cream and bacon), **amatriciana** (bacon, pecorino cheese and tomatoes), **vongole** (clams in oil and garlic), **frutte di mare** (mixed seafood in tomato sauce) and in season, sautéed porcini mushrooms.

In Vino Veritas
Sample and take home
Italy's excellent wines
from one of the the
following *enotecas*.
• **Enoteca Capranica**,
✉ piazza Capranica
104, ☎ 06 6994-0992.
Combines simple cui-
sine with wine tasting.
• **Al Vino al Vino**,
✉ via dei Serpenti 19,
☎ 06 485-803.
Over 500 wines along
with various spirits,
Sicilian food and attrac-
tive surroundings.
• **Il Goccetto**,
✉ via dei Banchi Vecchi
14, ☎ 06 686-4268.
Excellent list of wines,
a convivial, clubby
atmosphere in a
medieval Bishop's
palace, and cheese
and salads to eat.
• **Trimani**,
✉ via Goito 20,
☎ 06 446-9661.
Reputed to be Rome's
oldest wine store.
Excellent selection.
• **Antica Enoteca di
Via della Croce**,
✉ via della Croce 76B,
☎ 06 679-7544.
Offers a choice of
many wines.

Do not expect **vegetables** with main dishes. There may be some French fries and perhaps a small garnish, but rarely more. *Contorni* (vegetables) are ordered separately. Favourites include *spinaci* (spinach), usually served with garlic and oil, or deep-fried chunks of *zucchini* (cour-gettes). An *insalata mista* (mixed salad), the most popular request, invariably incor-porates lettuce-type leaves with *rucciola* (rocket) and tomato.

Don't miss out on the excellent **cheeses** Italy produces. Apart from the well-known standards such as *parmigiano* (parmesan), *gorgonzola* or *bel paese*, ask for *pecorino* (a hard cheese made of sheep's milk), *taleg-gio* (pungent, softish cheese) and *grana* (a cousin to *parmigiano*).

Romans are not really big on **desserts** but there is always a selection of *gelati* (ice cream) available for sale, or a delicious *tiramisù*, and sometimes you will be able to find a *crostata di ricotta* (a tasty local cheesecake). There is also a good selection of seasonal fruit, which marries well with cheese and is an excellent way to round off a meal.

What to Drink

In Italy, **wine** is considered an essential accompaniment to any meal. The nearest wine-producing region to Rome is the Castelli Romani district, which produces dry white wines. Look out for Frascati, Velletri and Grottaferrata, as many of the house wines offered in restaurants by the carafe come from here. Pinot Grigio (from the Veneto) and Vernaccia (from Tuscany) are also two light, white wines. The best red

wines come from northern Italy, and the wines to look for here are the full-bodied rich Barolo, Barbaresco or Nebbiolo. Chianti is a popular, and sometimes excellent, wine from Tuscany. *Aqua minerale* (mineral water), either *frizzante* or *naturale*, is widely available. Ferrarelle, San Pellegrino and San Benedetto are popular varieties of sparkling water.

Italy also produces some very drinkable beers. Nastro Azzurro, Peroni and Moretti are among the most popular here, although internationally renowned beers are also widely available. If you prefer draught beer, ask for a *birra alla spina*.

Wine Production

Italy is the world's second largest wine producer, with a growing industry. Small wine holdings proliferate, the number of DOC areas (**Denominazione d'Origine Controlata**, the system for categorizing wine by area and ensuring quality) has increased and more attention is being given to producing high-quality wines than the traditional *vino di tavola* (table wines). Indeed, the finest red wines compete with the best in the world, but they are pricing themselves out of the ordinary wine-drinkers' market. However, wine lovers are now watching the so-called 'emerging regions', the newer DOCs in the east of Italy.

Fettuccine all' Alfredo
One of Italy's great pasta dishes, glorified by the likes of **Douglas Fairbanks** and **Mary Pickford**, is *Fettuccine all' Alfredo*. It was invented in 1925 by owner-chef **Alfredo**, of the famous **Alfredo alla Scrofa** restaurant. Although the recipe remains a house secret, home-made *fettuccine* ribbon noodles are served on a specially heated plate coated in Alfredo's sauce of pure butter, finest *parmigiano* and … he's keeping mum about the rest of the ingredients.

Below: *Cocktails are part of summer indulgences.*

• *LUXURY*
Quinzi & Gabrieli
Reputed for elegant clientele, and fabulous fish and seafood dishes. Near Pantheon and Piazza Navona. Dinner only.
✉ *via delle Coppelle 6*,
☎ *06 687-9389*.

Checchino dal 1887
Renowned Roman restaurant in the Testaccio area.
✉ *via di Monte Testaccio 30*,
☎ *06 574-6318*,
💻 *www.checchino-dal-1887.com*

Agata e Romeo
One of the city's leading restaurants; innovative and ever-changing menu.
✉ *via Carlo Alberto 45*, ☎ *06 446-6115*.

Piperno
One of Rome's best-known restaurants, featuring Jewish dishes; in a square tucked behind the Palazzo de Cenci.
✉ *via Monte dei Cenci 9*,
☎ *06 6880-6629*.

La Rosetta
This is still considered to be Rome's best fish restaurant. Bustling.
✉ *via della Rosetta 3*,
☎ *06 686-1002*.

Les Etoiles
Star-rated, innovative Italian cuisine; fabulous views toward St Peter's.
✉ *Hotel Atlante Star*.

• *MID-RANGE*
Da Giggetto
In the shadow of ancient Rome, good Jewish cuisine. Renowned for its artichoke dishes.
✉ *via del Portico d'Ottavia 21/a*,
☎ *06 686-1105*,
💻 *www. giggettoalportico.com*

Baires
A touch of Argentina in the heart of Rome. Great steaks, fine *empanadas*, imported wines and a good Latin atmosphere.
✉ *corso Rinascimento 1*,
☎ *06 686-1293;*
✉ *via Cavour 315*,
☎ *06 6920-2164*.

Osteria dell'Antiquario

A small, intimate restaurant. Outdoor dining; Mediterranean cuisine.
⊠ *piazza di San Simeone 26/27,*
☎ *06 687-9694.*

Cannavota

Traditional Italian food; patronized by many locals.
⊠ *piazza San Giovanni in Laterano 20,* ☎ *06 7720-5007.*

Ai Tre Scalini

Creative Mediterranean cuisine just behind Colosseum.
⊠ *via dei SS Quattro 30,* ☎ *06 709-6309.*

Alfredo a Via Gabi

Fine restaurant just outside the city walls.
⊠ *via Gabi 38,*
☎ *06 7720-6792.*

Roof Garden

Great views and Italian cuisine.
⊠ *Hotel Forum.*

Antico Caffè della Pace

Ivy-draped building in a quiet side street serving drinks and snacks. Restaurant also available behind.
⊠ *Piazza della Pace,*
☎ *06 686-1216.*

Terra di Siena

Bright and innovative restaurant serving Tuscan fare.
⊠ *piazza Pasquino 77/78,* ☎ *06 6830-7704.*

Osteria Margutta

Pretty street restaurant, interesting décor, with good Roman fare. Inexpensive to moderate.
⊠ *via Margutta 82,*
☎ *06 323-1025.*

Gino in Vicolo Rosini

A good restaurant just behind parliament. Inexpensive to moderate.
⊠ *vicolo Rosini 4,*
☎ *06 687-3434.*

Margutta Vegetariano

State-of-the-art vegetarian restaurant with up-market décor.
⊠ *via Margutta 118,*
☎ *06 3265-0577.*

Caffè Rosati

Fine historic café restaurant, with pavement terrace, bar-café, patisserie downstairs and restaurant upstairs. Perfect for the summer months.
⊠ *piazza del Popolo 4/5/5a,* ☎ *06 322-5859.*

Ristorante Armando al Pantheon

Fine neighbourhood restaurant serving local cuisine.
⊠ *via salita del Crescenzi 31*
☎ *06 6880-3034.*

Spirito di Vino

Historic Medieval building (where the Classical sculpture of the Apoxiomenos was discovered), with fine Roman cuisine.
⊠ *vicolo dell' Atleta 13, or via dei Genovesi 31B,* ☎ *06 589-6689.*

Riparte Café

Restaurant, grill, music bar and exhibition venue with innovative cuisine.
⊠ *via degli Orti di Trastevere 1,*
☎ *06 586-1816.*

Romolo nel Giardino della Fornarina

Historic setting with Roman cuisine.
✉ via di Porta Settimiana 8,
☎ 06 581-8284.

Il Tinello

Popular *trattoria* and *pizzeria* near Villa Borghese park.
✉ via di Porta Pinciana 16/B, ☎ 06 48-6847.

Planet Hollywood

Movies and meals.
✉ via del Tritone 118,
☎ 06 4282-8012.

Hard Rock Café

Burgers, loud music, expensive souvenirs.
✉ via Veneto 62a,
☎ 06 420-3051.

Alfredo alla Scrofa

This is where *fettucine all' Alfredo* was invented back in 1925. Still going strong.
✉ via della Scrofa 104,
☎ 06 6880-6163.

'Gusto

Trendy, minimalist wine bar, *pizzeria* and restaurant, with a bookstore, live music and Sunday brunch specials.
✉ piazza Augusto Imperatore 9,
☎ 06 322-6273.

Supperclub

The antithesis of the backstreet *trattoria*, this is the ultimate modern evening out – dinner lounging on Roman mattresses, live performances, DJs, and even a massage between courses.
✉ Via dei Nari,
☎ 06 6880-7207.

La Taverna del Ghetto Kosher

Kosher restaurant serving traditional Roman Jewish cuisine. Closed Fri dinner.
✉ via del Portico d'Ottavia 7B/8,
☎ 06 6880-9771.

Hosteria Antica Roma

Alfresco dining by candlelight amid the ruins on the Appian Way. Roman and Mediterranean specialities, with authentic ancient Roman recipes on Tue and Thu.
✉ Via Clementi III,
☎ 06 627-9862.

Enoteca Capranica

A fine *enoteca* (good choice of wines), *pizzeria* and restaurant in a beautifully restored old palazzo.
✉ piazza Capranica 99, ☎ 06 6994-0992.

• *BUDGET*
Mary Meeting

Near Piazza Venezia, a large inexpensive restaurant; Roman-style cuisine. Plenty of pastas.
✉ via Genova 20/22,
☎ 06 488-1396.

Sora Margherita

Small and homely; some traditional Jewish Roman dishes. No credit cards.
✉ piazza delle Cinque Scole 30,
☎ 06 686-4002.

La Pollarola dell' Omo

Old family-run *trattoria* with Roman fare. Lunch only.
✉ piazza Pollarola 24,
☎ 06 6880-1654.

Trattoria da Gino e Pietro

Excellent pastas and salads, just behind Piazza Navona.
✉ *via del Governo Vecchio 106,*
☎ *06 686-1576.*

I Tre Scalini

A café-*gelateria* with a long-standing reputation.
✉ *piazza Navona 28-32,* ☎ *06 6880-1996.*

Giolitti

Renowned *gelateria*, café and *pasticceria*.
✉ *via Uffici del Vicario 40,* ☎ *06 699-1243.*

Caffè Novecento

Enoteca and *Sala di Té*, in a renovated, historic building; good wines, cold dishes and tea and pastries.
✉ *via del Governo Vecchio 12,*
☎ *06 686-5242.*

Osteria del Gallo

Pretty restaurant in quiet street; small but good Roman menu.
✉ *vicolo di Montevecchio 27,*
☎ *06 687-3781.*

Buon Sapore

A popular Chinese restaurant with indoor seating and take-away facilities.
✉ *via della Palombella 34-35,* ☎ *06 6813-5318.*

Fabrizio

Homely Trastevere *trattoria* with good Roman fare.
✉ *via Santa Dorotea 15,* ☎ *06 580-6244.*

Edy

Good Roman *trattoria* in a small side street.
✉ *vicolo del Babuino 4,* ☎ *06 3600-1738.*

Il Re degli Amici

Friendly *trattoria* with traditional fare.
✉ *via della Croce 33/B,* ☎ *06 679-5380.*

Otello alla Concordia

A traditional *osteria*, excellent menu.
✉ *via della Croce 81,*
☎ *06 679-1178.*

Pancotto in Trastevere

Traditional Roman cuisine, pizza and an array of desserts.

Pavement terrace.
✉ *viale Trastevere 8,*
☎ *06 580-6334.*

Peperone

A bargain on fashionable Via Veneto.
✉ *via Veneto 97,*
☎ *06 488-4592.*

Il Brillo Parlante

Good wines, excellent lunches in a pricey part of town.
✉ *via della Fontanella 12,* ☎ *06 324-3334.*

Al Gambero 2

Cheap, cheerful and popular.
✉ *corner Via Belsiana and Via della Croce,*
☎ *06 678-2696.*

Al 34

Excellent Roman *trattoria* with a good reputation; in the centre.
✉ *via Mario de' Fiori 34,* ☎ *06 679-5091.*

Al Pompiere

An attractive, first-floor *osteria* with a fine tradition for Roman food.
✉ *via Santa Maria dei Calderari 38,*
☎ *06 686-8377.*

Above: *The Rome Film Fest, usually in October, is a must for all movie-lovers.*

ENTERTAINMENT
Nightlife

Much of Rome's nightlife is traditional – dining out, drinking in a café, bar or *enoteca* – but there are some excellent pubs, clubs and discos, not always in the centre, that pack in the crowds from autumn to early summer (they close in mid-summer as clubbers head for Ostia and the coast) and a wide range of concerts, plays, opera and ballet, as befits an international city. The Thursday edition of *La Repubblica* produces a weekly supplement, *Trovaroma*, which lists, in Italian, what's on in town. In summer, a number of monuments (such as the Colosseum) have occasional performances or exhibitions at night.

The inexpensive weekly publication, *Roma c'è* (in Italian), and the fortnightly, *un Ospite a Roma* offer up-to-date entertainment listings in both Italian and English. The publication *Evento*, published by the Comune di Roma, is in both Italian and English and can be found in most hotels.

Cinema

Movies are usually in Italian, but English or original language films are shown at **Warner Village Moderno**, ⊠ piazza della Repubblica 45; **Intrastevere**, ⊠ viale Moroni 3 (Trastevere); **Eden Film Center**, ⊠ piazza Cola di Rienzo 74; and **Metropolitan**, ⊠ via del Corso 7. They are also shown on some nights of the week at the **Nuovo Sacher**, ⊠ largo Aschianghi 1, and the **Alcazar**, ⊠ via Cardinale Merry del Val 14.

Annual Events

Although there are few religious events, there are plenty of traditional ones. Among the most enjoyable are the **Festa della Primavera**, at the end of March, when the Spanish Steps are decked out with thousands of pots of azaleas. In June, the spectacular **Festa dei Fiori** (flower festival) takes place in Genzano, in the Castelli Romani. Either side of the Tiber banks, between Castel San Angelo and Via Cavour, the **Expo Tevere** brings a colourful display of regional arts and crafts along with mouthwatering food products to central Rome from mid-June to mid-July. The **Festa di Noantri** is celebrated in Trastevere with processions and feasts during the last two weeks in July. An **Arts Fair** is held in Via Margutta during September, and a **Crafts Fair** in Via dell' Orso during the last week of September. Also from the end of September is the month-long **RomaEuropa** performing arts festival.

The other major festival to look out for is the **Estate Romana**, a summer-long arts festival held in outdoor venues across the city. There are classical concerts in gardens and historical sites such as the Baths of Caracalla, jazz and blues music in piazzas and theatre in the ruins at Ostia Antica, and the Foro Italico becomes the spot for rock concerts and discos. Also on offer are night-time archaeological visits and outdoor movie screenings.

> **Primo Maggio**
> This big rock concert, organized by Italy's biggest labour unions, takes place annually on 1 May in front of the Basilica di San Giovanni in Laterano – a rather odd setting for loud rock music. Thousands gather to hear great local and international acts. If you are in Rome in May, be sure not to miss this one.

Below: *During the summer, the Colosseum has exhibits at night.*

Right: *The
Auditorium Parco
della Musica is a
favourite spot for
musicals and theatre.*

Theatre

Plays are an important part of Rome's entertainment and arts life, and with performances being played out in over 80 theatres, as well as at historic locations, the theatre-goer in Rome is spoiled for choice.

For classic theatre visit the **Teatro Argentina**, **Valle**, and **Nazionale**, where famous actors offer high quality performances. Another theatre to look out for is the **Ghione Theatre**, located on one side of St Peter's Square. This 600-seat venue offers classical plays as well as musical concerts. For something less traditional be sure to stop at the **Abraxa Teatro** for avant-garde physical theatre. If, however, your mood is slightly lighter, the **Teatro della Cometa** and the **Teatro Flaiano** offer light comedies, and the **Sistina** offers a wide selection of musicals.

English-language productions are on show at the **Teatro Olimpico**, **L'Arciliuto Teatro** and the **Forum**. **The Miracle Players**, a company of English-speaking players, put on performances at various historic locations during the summer.

The theatre season lasts from October to May, but often continues throughout the summer months. Ticket reservations for all listed theatres ☎ 06 8530-1758.

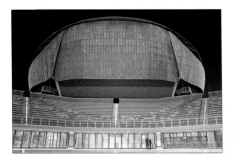

Left: *During the summer ballets are performed at the Baths of Caracalla.*

Dance

Throughout the year there are a number of opportunities to see dance performances. In the summer months various dance companies tour through the city giving performances at outdoor dance festivals. The **RomaEuropa Festival** at the end of September offers modern dance productions and the summer-long **Estate Romana** also has a few dance programmes.

Ballet is becoming more popular in Rome and although the audience attendance will never be staggering, the big classic ballets can sell out. A performance usually runs for three to six nights and on the first night guest stars perform the leading roles. The remaining shows are performed by the company's own dancers. The **Corpo di Ballo del Teatro dell'Opera di Roma** performs several ballets a year in the **Teatro dell'Opera**, and some smaller, new pieces are performed in a smaller venue (usually the Teatro Nazionale). The Teatro dell'Opera also has a summer programme – ballets are performed outdoors at the **Baths of Caracalla**.

Termi di Caracalla
Better known as the site of historic concerts, this large complex was started by Emperor Caracalla in AD212, but was finished only after his death. It was conceived to be what we would think of today as a huge leisure drome – a fitness centre with gardens, libraries and recreational areas capable of housing 1600 people – for the Romans believed that the body and the mind should be kept in trim. Remains of the *caldarium* (hot baths) can be seen on the exterior; the huge arches protecting the *tepidarium* (warm baths) and *frigidarium* (cold baths), and parts of the gymnasia, are all distinguishable. Some of the finest sculptures found here are now part of the Farnese Collection in the Archaeological Museum in Naples.

Above: *Live music plays a big part in everyday Roman life.*

Tickets and Seating at the Teatro dell'Opera
Although you buy tickets individually, the majority of seats are in boxes, so you could share with strangers. Therefore, queues start forming early. Some of the boxes higher up can be very cheap, and good-value seats are in the top-level Galleria and in the Balconata beneath. People under 25 and over 65 qualify for half-price tickets, but not for first nights and on the cheapest seats. If buying on the day of the production, you save a 10% booking fee. Prices also vary depending on the production – first nights are usually more expensive and the summer season can be quite cheap.

Music

Live music is very popular in Rome. From rock, pop and dance music to classical music and opera, the city caters for every taste.

For the young at heart, Rome has a wide array of live music venues offering jazz and blues bands and DJs playing dance music. For more information, *see* the listings on pages 76–77.

Classical music lovers will find a wide array of concerts, from chamber music at the **Accademia di Santa Cecilia** to Baroque music concerts at the **Gonfalone**. Other venues for classical music (and opera) include the **Accademia Filarmonica Romana** and **Il Tempietto**. During the summer months concerts are also held at outdoor locations like the **Baths of Caracalla**. Check with a travel agent, hotel or buy an entertainment guide to see the time and place of the concerts. Many churches, including **San Nicola in Carcere**, **Sant'Ignazio**, **Chiesa Valdese** and **Sant'Eustachio**, also have live classical music performances.

Opera is an Italian specialty. In the summer months outdoor operas are held at the

Basilica San Clemente and, in recent years, the **Stadio Olimpico**. The summer venues change from year to year, so it would be best to buy an entertainment guide and check out the venues before going.

The opera season runs from November/December to May and although some classical music venues (*see* previous page) offer opera performances, the undisputed home of opera is the **Teatro dell'Opera**. Remember, though, that Italians dress up for performances, so in order to blend in, rather dress up than down. Also take note that Saturday and Sunday performances take place early (18:00 on a Saturday and 17:00 on a Sunday) and there are usually no performances on a Monday. The **Teatro Nazionale** and the **Teatro Brancaccio** also offer opera performances.

Spectator Sports

Rome, like the rest of Italy, is obsessed with **football**. The city's two top-level sides, **S.S. Lazio** and **A.S. Roma**, both play in Italy's 'Serie A' and the matches are something to behold. If during your stay you get the opportunity to see a game, don't hesitate – it is well worth it. As the stadium vibrates from the sound of thousands of supporters cheering and chanting, cast your mind back to the gladiatorial games of yore, because this spectacle is probably the modern-day equivalent.

Both teams play at the **Stadio Olimpico** on alternate weeks (unless of course they are playing each other). For information on S.S. Lazio ☎ 06 323-7333, and for A.S. Roma ☎ 06 6920-0642. Also *see* page 41 for more information on other sports and recreation.

Music Venues
Accademia di Santa Cecilia
⊠ via della Conciliazione 4
☎ 06 6880-1044

Il Gonfalone
⊠ via del Gonfalone 32A
☎ 06 687-5952

Accademia Filarmonica Romana
⊠ via Flamini 118
☎ 06 320-1752

Il Tempietto
⊠ via Rodolfo Morandi 3
☎ 06 2332-26360

San Nicola in Carcere
⊠ via del Teatro di Marcello 46
☎ 06 6830-7198

Sant'Ignazio
⊠ Piazza S. Ignazio, via del Caravita 8A

Chiesa Valdese
⊠ via Marianna Dionig 57i
☎ 06 320-4868

Basilica San Clemente
⊠ via Labicana 95
☎ 06 7045-1018

Teatro Brancaccio
⊠ via Merulana 244
☎ 06 4782-4893

Stadio Olimpico
⊠ Via del Foro Italico
☎ 06 323-7910

Bars, Pubs & Nightclubs
Goa
Perennial favourite with live performers.
⊠ via Libetta 13,
☎ 06 574-8277.

Zoo Bar
Popular favourite for its varied music styles, now in a new location.
⊠ via Bencivenga 1,
☎ 339-272-7995.

Metaverso
Another popular venue.
⊠ via Monte Testaccio 38a,
☎ 06 574-4722.

Trinity College
Irish pub meets disco. A gathering place for Anglophones.
⊠ via del Collegio Romano 6,
☎ 06 678-6472.

Alexanderplatz
Rome's favourite jazz club with restaurant.
⊠ via Osita 9,
☎ 06 3975-1877.

Charity Café
Ideal for tea by day and wine and jazz by night.
⊠ via Panisperna 68,
☎ 06 7030-5684.

Stardust
Tiny bar, but very popular with late-night revelers. Plays a mix of music, from rock to opera, from rap to Cuban jazz. Gets really raucous after 23:00.
⊠ vicolo de'Renzi 4,
☎ 06 5832-0875,
🛆 Entrance free; no credit cards.
🕐 19:00–02:00 Mon–Sat; noon–02:00 Sun.

Right: *The Hard Rock Café is still a popular restaurant-bar in Rome.*

Akab

Busy club with underground cellar, plus garden for summer months. Tuesday nights are very popular.
✉ *via di Monte Testaccio 68-69,*
☎ *06 5725-0585,*
💰 *€10–€20 (including one drink),*
🕐 *23:00–04:00. Closed Jul and Aug.*

Big Mama

Popular blues club with array of Italian and international artists. Food is also served – book early to ensure a table.
✉ *vicolo San Francesco a Ripa 18,*
☎ *06 581-2551,*
💰 *Free with membership (annual €13, monthly €8); extra for big acts,*
🕐 *21:00–01:30 Tue–Sat. Closed early Jun–Sep.*

Caruso-Caffè de Oriente

Latin American music every night except Saturdays. Live acts almost daily. A must for salsa lovers.
✉ *via di Monte Testaccio 36,*
☎ *06 574-5019,*
💰 *€8–€15 (including one drink),*
🕐 *22:30–03:30 Tue–Thu, Sun; 23:00–04:30 Fri, Sat. Closed mid-June to mid-Sep.*

Alpheus

Eclectic club with varied crowd. Has four big halls for live music, music festivals, theatre and cabaret. Music changes every night as well as from room to room.
✉ *via del Commercio 36,* ☎ *06 574-7826,*
💰 *€5–€20,*
🕐 *22:00–04:00 Fri–Sun. Closed Jul–Aug.*

Micca

One of Rome's newest clubs. Has themed party nights and Sunday night jazz. Sign on-line guest book to get in.
✉ *via Pietro Micca 7, Porto Maggiore,*
☎ *06 8744-0079,*
🕐 *22:00–03:00 Thu–Sat, 18:00–03:00 Sun*
M *Vittorio/Manzoni*
🖳 *www.miccaclub.com*

Wine Bars

Gusto
✉ piazza Augusto Imperatore 9
☎ 06 322-6273

Enoteca Cavour
✉ via Cavour 31
☎ 06 678-5496

Vinarium
✉ via dei Volsci 103/107
☎ 06 446-2110

L'Orange
✉ piazza Ippolito Nievo 15/16, on Viale di Trastevere
☎ 06 5830-0238

Al Vino Al Vino
✉ via dei Serpenti 19
☎ 06 485-803

Le Passaggiata

A fun and free pastime, Le Passaggiata, or the evening stroll, is enjoyed by locals and tourists alike. After dinner, people stroll across the piazzas, meeting and greeting fellow strollers. It is the perfect opportunity to see and be seen. If you want to blend in, wear something fashionable – the Italians take care to look their best. Popular places to walk are the Via Condotti, Piazza di Spagna, Via del Corso and Piazza Navona.

Above: *A bust of Hadrian, the great emperor and architect.*

EXCURSIONS

Much of modern Rome extends beyond the ancient city walls, and within the urban area there are still many important sights for the tourist. The large park area of **Villa Borghese** (*see* page 26), just behind Villa Medici and Via Veneto, houses three top museums in its **Museo Borghese**, **Villa Giulia** and the **Museo d'Arte Moderna** (*see* page 39). The leafy park, itself, brings a breath of welcome fresh air to the city centre.

Another historic villa surrounded by a park is the **Villa Doria Pamphilj**, country residence of the Doria Pamphilj families. The extensive grounds are a popular recreational spot with families and children.

The magnificent basilica of **San Paolo fuori le Mura** (St Paul's beyond the Walls) is well worth the bus or taxi ride for its lovely cloisters, although much of its interior has been rebuilt.

Further afield, but accessible on a day trip, there are more remains of Ancient Rome. The **catacombs**, of which there are a number on the outskirts of the city, were used to bury early Christians, while **Ostia Antica**, the remains of Rome's port on the Tirrenian Sea, is also a fascinating place to visit.

Seeking respite from the sometimes hot summers, **Hadrian** looked to the hills and, in the middle of the Roman countryside just below the town of Tivoli, constructed his villa and started a trend amongst later rulers, including the popes. The once beautiful **Villa d'Este**, in the heart of modern Tivoli, was built in the 16th century and has wonderful water gardens and grottoes.

Castel Gandolfo
In the **Alban Hills** just 25km (15 miles) south of Rome, and overlooking crater **Lake Albano**, is the small town of **Castel Gandolfo**, better known as the summer residence of the Pontiff. The palazzo in which the Pope stays was built by **Carlo Maderno** in 1624 for **Pope Urban VIII** and was enlarged by subsequent rulers. None of the papal properties are open to the public but the town is very pleasant and the setting, impressive.

Villa Doria Pamphilj and Gardens

A modest bus-ride beyond Trastevere will take you to the gates of one of Rome's largest recreational areas – the Villa Doria Pamphilj and its surrounding parklands.

Created by **Pope Innocenzo X** – a Pamphilj – the Villa Doria Pamphilj is an immense area of greenery, providing lungs to urban Rome. So large and so varied is the topography of this park that one is inclined to forget that it is located in the heart of one of Europe's capital cities. At weekends, it is particularly popular with families and joggers. The villa dates back to the mid-17th century when the pope commissioned **Alessandro Algardi** and **Giovanni Francesco Grimaldi** to build a residence for his nephew, Camillo Pamphilj. It was modified in the 18th century by **Prince Filippo Andrea V Doria Pamphilj** and much of what we see today is the result of this remodelling. Following extensive renovation, the villa's various formal gardens are now open to the public.

> **Villa Doria Pamphilj and Gardens**
> **Location:** Map E–C4
> **Distance from city:** 30km (19 miles)
> ✉ Via Aurelia Antica
> ☎ 06 679-7323
> ⏰ 09:00–19:00 Tue–Sun
>
> **Villa Giulia**
> **Location:** Map E–E4
> **Distance from city:** 30km (19 miles)
> ✉ piazzale di Villa Giulia 9
> ☎ 06 322-6571
> ⏰ 09:00–19:00 Tue–Sun

Villa Giulia

Another country residence, the Villa Giulia was constructed by **Vignola**, **Vasari** and **Ammannati** for **Pope Julius III** in 1550. Its particular interest lies in the **nymphaeum**, a sunken courtyard in Classical style, the reproduction of an **Etruscan Temple**, and the magnificent collection of Etruscan artefacts from a tomb at **Cerveteri** (dating back to the 8th century BC) that form the **Museo Nazionale Etrusco** (see page 39).

Below: *The Villa Giulia has a priceless collection of Etruscan artefacts, such as this 2500-year-old vase.*

Catacombe de San Calllisto
Location: Map E–D4
Distance from city:
25km (16 miles)
🚌 Bus 118/218
✉ via Appia Antica 110
☎ 06 5130-1580
🕐 Closed Wednesday
🖳 www.
catacombe.roma.it

Basilica de San Sebastiano
Location: Map E–D4
Distance from city:
25km (16 miles)
🚌 Bus 118
✉ Via Appia
☎ 06 785-0350
🕐 09:00–12:00,
14:00–17:00

Le Catacombe (The Catacombs)

Rome is surrounded by catacombs. These underground tunnels, hewn out of the soft, volcanic tufa rock, provided meeting places and burial sites for early Christians during the time they were still persecuted.

The **Catacombe de San Callisto** are among the several catacombs along the Via Appia that are open to visitors. It was here that St Cecilia was entombed, and excavations have revealed the remains of hundreds of thousands of people in its kilometres of corridors. The **Basilica de San Sebastiano** was built over the catacombs where, among others, the remains of saints Paul and Peter were once kept.

San Paolo fuori le Mura

A fire in 1823 destroyed much of the original basilica and what we see today, impressive though it at first appears, is a heavily restored version, a modern copy or – in the case of the entrance quadrangle – far later additions. There are, however, some exceptions.

The marble canopy over the altar is a beautiful work by 13th-century sculptor **Arnolfo di Cambio**, while below the altar are the remains of a 1st-century tomb, possibly St Paul's; some of the frescoes are vestiges of the work of **Pietro Cavallini**; the handsome pascal candlestick is a 12th-century work by **Niccolò di Angelo** and **Pietro Vassalletto**. The only parts to escape fire were the magnificent cloisters, which belonged to the Benedictine convent adjacent. Have a

Below: *The relatively modern exterior of San Paolo fuori le Mura.*

look at the delicate paired twisted columns – absolute masterpieces of Medieval decoration – and the courtyard, which dates from the early 13th century.

Ostia Antica

Ostia Antica enjoyed over 650 years of importance as the port serving the **Roman Empire** and was then cast aside during Constantine's rule in favour of Porto, a newer facility built to the north. After its commercial decline and endemic malaria, Ostia (which once boasted a population of nearly 100,000) was practically abandoned and ultimately became silted up with sand. Thanks to this undisturbed silt, when serious excavations began a century ago, this ancient port was found to have been well preserved.

Ostia Antica's importance today lies with the discovery of its commercial and domestic architecture, consisting of various apartments and small houses. There are also a number of individual villas such as the **Casa di Diana**. As Rome's vernacular architecture has largely disappeared, the discoveries at contemporary Ostia are of immense value to archaeologists.

The **Porta Romana** leads into the town's main street, **Decumanus Maximus**, running through the centre and down to the Porta Marina, the old city gate on the seafront. The ground plans of Terme di Nettuno, or Neptune's Baths, a theatre which has been renovated for performances, offices of the various guilds, and the Forum are all clearly

Above: *A view of Ostia Antica archaeological site.*

San Paolo fuori le Mura
Location: Map E–D4
Distance from city: 15km (9 miles)
✉ via Ostiense 186
☎ 06 541-0341
🕐 07:30–18:30

Ostia Antica
Location: Map E–B5
Distance from city: 30 minutes from Rome
Ⓜ Train from Termini station. Stop before Lido di Ostia.
🕐 Ruins open Jan/Feb/Nov/Dec 08:30–16:00; Mar 08:30–17:00; Apr–Oct 08:30–18:00
♿ €4

Casa di Diana
☎ 06 785-0350

discernible. The grain warehouses, *horrea*, are also well preserved. The temple of Roma and Augustus dates back to the 1st century AD and there are also a number of smaller places of worship (a synagogue and Mithran temples) that confirm the spirit of religious tolerance prevalent in Ostia Antica.

Less classically inclined visitors who want to escape the summer heat and spend a bit of time at the beach can catch a train for the fast 31km (20-mile) trip to Ostia where, on the **Tyrrhenian Sea**, the **Lido di Ostia** is a popular resort with full beach facilities and plenty of restaurants. The sea is not the cleanest in Italy but it does at least offer an alternative to hot city days.

EUR

This area has now become a **satellite town** to Rome. It is easily reachable either by bus or by metro and provides a different view of the city. EUR was begun in 1938 for the **Esposizione Universale di Roma**, which was to have been held in Rome in 1942 (but was cancelled because of World War II). It was taken up again after the war and the area developed into one for both residential and administrative use. Today you'll find an excellent, large shopping centre, **Cinecittà 2** (which has some very good shops), a couple of **museums** (the Museum of Prehistory and Ethnography Luigi Pigorini and the Museum of Roman Civilization), and the **Palazzo della Civiltà del Lavoro**, which, with its arched recesses, is known locally as the **Square Colosseum**.

EUR
Location: Map E–D4
Distance from city: 40km from the city

Cinecittà 2
⊠ viale Palmiro Toglia 2
🕐 Mon–Fri 10:00–20:00; Sat 09:30–20:30; Sun 10:00–20:00
Ⓜ EUR Fermi

Palazzo della Civiltà del Lavoro
⊠ piazza G Agnelli 10
🕐 09:00–18:45. Closed Monday.
Ⓜ EUR Fermi

Museum of Prehistory and Ethnography
⊠ viale Lincoln 1
🕐 09:00–14:00; 09:00–13:00 Sun. Closed Monday

Museum of Roman Civilization
⊠ piazza Giovanni Agnelli 10
🕐 09:00–19:00. Closed Monday.
Ⓜ EUR Fermi

Into the Castelli Romani

For a long day's excursion out of Rome, there is a round trip through the area known as the Castelli Romani. This area is essentially **volcanic** and on many of the hill tops you'll see the remains of fortresses and towers, built in the Middle Ages by noble families intent on securing their territory. They used the volcanic craters as a safe 'wall' against possible intruders and today, as well as the ruins, there are also some pretty lakes to discover.

The fertile soil is ideal for this area's active viticultural industry, bottling wine under the Castelli Romani label. The most famous is the white wine, Frascati, named for the Castelli Romani village from which it comes. In Frascati, visit the **Villa Aldobrandini** designed by Giacomo della Porta but built for the Cardinal by Carlo Maderno and completed in 1603. A highlight of this villa is its garden and the views from it. Another well-known local wine comes from Grottaferrata which is also the site of the important monastery, the **Abbazia Greca San Nilo di Grottaferrata**, built by Greek monks in the 11th century. Its museum is full of interesting ecclesiastical exhibits.

On the slopes near **Lake Nemi** lies the town of **Genzano di Roma**, renowned for its sumptuous floral festival each June. Here in the town's Via Belardi the **Infiorata** takes place. The street is transformed into a floral canvas, decked out in multicoloured designs from pavement to pavement with billions of flower heads.

Castelli Romani
Location: Map E–E5
Distance from city:
25km (16 miles)

Villa Aldobrandini
✉ via Mazzarino 1
☎ 06 678-7864

Abbazia Greca San Nilo di Grottaferrata
✉ corso del Popolo 128
☎ 06 945-9309
🕐 08:30–12:00, 16:00–18:00

Opposite: *Originally built for the Esposizione Universale di Roma, the EUR has become a district of Rome, with good shopping.*
Below: *The Villa Aldobrandini has beautiful gardens.*

Above: *Police officers on horseback are a familiar sight in Rome.*

Tourist Information

The **Italian State Tourist Office** (🖳 www.enit.it) operates in a number of major cities including: **UK**, ✉ 1 Princes Street, London, W1B 2AY, ☎ (020) 7408 1254; **Australia**, ✉ Level 4, 46 Market Street, Sydney, ☎ (02) 9262 1666; **Canada**, ✉ South Tower, Suite 907, 175 Bloor St, Toronto M4W 3R8, Ontario, ☎ (416) 925 4882; **New York**, ✉ 630 Fifth Avenue, Suite 1565, NY 100111, ☎ (212) 245-4822, (offices also in Chicago and Los Angeles). Check out 🖳 www.italiantourism.com for up-to-date information, and the Ministry of Culture at 🖳 www.beniculturali.it for information on the city's cultural sights. Alternatively, on arrival pick up a free city map and head for one of the following information centres: **APT** (the Rome tourism office), ✉ via Parigi 11, ☎ (06) 488-991, 🖳 www.romaturismo.it ⊕ 09:00–19:00, Mon–Sat. They also operate an office at the airport, ☎ (06) 65951, ⊕ 09:00–19:00 daily. **APT della Provincia di Roma** (covering the area surrounding Rome), ✉ via XX Settembre 26, ☎ (06) 421-3801, 🖳 www.aptprovroma.it **Informa Roma** run nine tourist information kiosks around town, ⊕ 09:30–19:30 daily. The most useful ones are at Castel Sant'Angelo ✉ Via del Tritone (second floor of La Rinascente), Termini station ✉ Via del Corso (Largo Goldoni) and Piazza Sonnino in Trastevere.

Entry Requirements

Visitors from EU countries require a valid national identity card or a passport – valid for a further six months after arrival. All other visitors require a valid passport. Most non EU citizens wishing to stay longer than 90 days will require a visa, as do some other nationals. If in doubt, check with your local embassy.

Customs

Customs regulations for goods bought duty-paid within the EU are fairly generous: 800 cigarettes, 200 cigars or 1kg (2.2lbs) tobacco, 10 litres (16 pints) spirits, 90 litres (120 standard bottles) wine and 100 litres (160 pints) of beer. For goods bought duty-free or outside the EU, the limits are: 400 cigarettes, 100 cigars, 1 litre spirits or 2 litres (just under 3 standard bottles) wine.

Getting There

By Air: Rome is directly linked to all major European cities and many towns in the USA. Direct flights from Rome also serve major cities in Asia and Australia. The flag carrier, **Alitalia**, ✉ via Alessandro Marchetti 111, ☎ 848-65642 (reservations), 8488-

65643 (information), 🖳 www.alitalia.com flies worldwide. Within Europe there are a number of popular low-cost airlines that serve the city, such as **EasyJet**, 🖳 www.easyjet.com, **Ryanair**, 🖳 www.ryanair.com, **Air Berlin** 🖳 www.airberlin.com and **BMI Baby**, 🖳 www.bmibaby.co.uk Other major international carriers with worldwide connections include: **British Airways**, ✉ via Bissolati 54, ☎ 199 712 260, 🖳 www.britishairways.com **Delta Airlines**, ✉ via Sardegna 40, ☎ 848 780 376, 🖳 www.delta.com **Lufthansa**, ✉ via di San Basilio 41, ☎ 199 499-0400, 🖳 www.lufthansa.com **Qantas**, ✉ via delle Città d'Europa, ☎ 848 359 010, 🖳 www.qantas.com and **Continental Airlines**, ✉ via Parigi 11, ☎ (06) 6605-3030, 🖳 www.continental.com **Fiumicino Airport:** This

is Rome's largest airport, officially known as Leonardo da Vinci di Fiumicino, ☎ (06) 6-5951 (switchboard), (06) 6595-3640 (information), 🖳 www.adr.it (combined website for Rome airports). Used by all major scheduled services, it is 26km (16 miles) southwest of the city centre.

Trains run every 20 minutes or so from Fiumicino Airport to central Rome. A direct train runs hourly (travel time 30 minutes) from Fiumicino to Stazione Termini, while a less expensive service runs every 20 minutes between Fiumicino and the suburbs of Trastevere, Ostiense and Tiburtina (travel time 60 minutes).

Taxis are available from Fiumicino to the centre of town (€40) and, for three travelling together, taxi is the cheapest option.

Ciampino Airport: Budget and charter flights tend to use Ciampino Airport, ☎ (06) 79-4941, 🖳

www.adr.it It is 15km (10 miles) southeast of the city centre. There are no direct trains from Ciampino Airport.
Airport Buses: From Fiumicino, Cotral (🖥 www.cotralspa.it), which also operates the subway system, offers bus services to the subway stations of Magliana and Lepanto – from which visitors can head to central Rome. From Ciampino, local buses run to the nearby Ciampino Town train station and the Anagnina Metro Station (at the start of Line A – which crosses Line B at Termini offering myriad connections), while EasyJet and Ryanair passengers can book a 40-minute ride on a bus directly into Stazione Termini, Rome, operated by Terravision (🖥 www.terravision.it). HR (Hotel Reservation, ☎ (06) 699-1000, 🖥 www. hotelreservation.it) offers in addition to a hotel reservation service, a minibus shuttle service to and from

both Rome airports. Likewise, there is a service offered by Airport Shuttle on 🖥 www.shuttle-airport. en/rome-airport Other buses connect the airport with Ciampino Town train station and Anagnina Metro Station, at the start of Metro Line A. This takes you via Termini – where lines A and B intersect – onward to the Spanish Steps and Vatican. Buses also run from Fiumicino to the subway stations of Magliana and Lepanto (travel time 60 minutes) every 30 minutes until 21:00. A taxi from Ciampino to the city centre should cost €30–35.
By Road: Travellers entering Italy by road from northern Europe can do so on toll highways (*autostrade*) from France (via Ventimiglia), various passes and tunnels through the Alps from Switzerland and Austria and, skirting Milan, can continue south on the A1, the

Autostrada del Sole to Rome. Non-resident cars are forbidden to drive through the historic centre. Visitors are advised to leave their cars in the outskirts or in one of the major car parks, such as Terminal Gianicolo, Via di Porta Cavalleggeri (Vaticano) and Terminal Park, via Marsala 30/32 (Stazione Termini) as parking in the capital is a nightmare. Visitors arriving by private car require insurance cover (an international Green Card) and must carry the vehicle's documents with them.
Renting a car for travel around the centre of Rome is not advisable, as the driving is lethal, theft is rife and parking non-existent. Care hire in Italy is also relatively expensive. The city's public transport system is more than adequate. For travellers heading out of Rome, the best deals are on the Internet. All the major car rental agencies are

present at the airport as well as downtown: **Avis** (airport, ☎ (06) 6501-1531); **Hertz** (airport, ☎ (06) 6501-0256) and **Europcar** (airport, ☎ (06) 6501-0879/977) are amongst the more popular at Fiumicino.

By Train: Rome's main station, Stazione Termini, has good railway connections with other Italian cities and onward connections to Switzerland, France, Belgium, Germany and the Netherlands. For tourists travelling through Italy (or Europe), one of the various rail passes can be a far more economic way of travelling the train routes. These include the **Inter-Rail Pass**, which is usually purchased in your home country (in the UK, contact **Rail Europe**, 🖥 www. raileurope.co.uk). For up-to-date train information look up the national trains website: 🖥 www.ferro viadellostato.it or 🖥 www.trenitalia.com Termini station has

decent restaurants, money exchange, hotel booking service, fast-food outlets and telephone facilities.

Money Matters

Currency: The Italian currency is the euro (€), split into 100 cents. A cup of coffee costs €1, a small bottle of mineral water at a kiosk, €1. The smallest coin is 1c; the most useful, the two-colour €1. Paper money starts with €5 and continues with 10, 20, 50, 100, 200 and 500 euro notes.

Exchange rates: The currency is now the same throughout the 12 countries of the Eurozone. Elsewhere, including the United Kingdom and United States, rates fluctuate on a daily basis, although they are relatively stable. Approximately, €1 is the equivalent of US$1.30, and worth about £0.60–£0.70 depending on the exchange. To exchange money, you can use one of the

Emergencies
If you are robbed, report the incident to the **Carabinieri** (military police) at their *caserma*, or **polizia** (civil police) at the *questura*, or telephone the emergency number ☎ 112. **Fire:** ☎ 115. **Breakdown** assistance on the road: ☎ 116. **Red Cross Ambulance** assistance: ☎ 118.
For medical assistance in English, *see* Health Services, on page 90.

Disabled Visitors
People are willing to help, but most facilities are poor and the area is full of steep hills and steps, cobbled or uneven streets and large areas with no access for cars. For information before you travel:
UK: RADAR (Royal Association for Disability and Rehabilitation) ✉ 12 City Forum, 250 City Road, London EC1V 8AF ☎ (020) 7250 4119 📠 (0171) 250 1212 🖥 www. radar.org.uk
Holiday Care Service, ✉ 2nd Floor, Imperial Buildings, Victoria Rd, Horley, Surrey RH6 7PZ ☎ 01293-774 535
USA: SATH (Society for the Advancement of Travel for the Handicapped) ✉ 347 Fifth Ave, Ste 610, New York NY10016 ☎ (212) 447 7284 🖥 www. sath.org

Best Times to Visit

Rome enjoys cool winters, warm spring and autumn weather, and summer days that can be uncomfortably hot and very crowded. The weather and the gardens are at their best in May and Jun, and Sep and Oct when the flora is in full leaf, and if it rains, it is rarely for long. Nov to Feb can be quite cold and rainy but the sights and transport are less crowded. Prices are at their highest from Easter until Nov, and again at Christmas. Jul and Aug are particularly crowded and a time when Romans, themselves, take a holiday, leaving *chiuso* (closed) notices on their shop and restaurant doors.

What to Pack

For the winter months, bring warm clothing, a collapsible umbrella and a light rain jacket. Budget and moderately priced hotels are not always well heated so bring warm bedding. Spring and autumn days can be either cool or warm so layered clothing is best. Summer clothing should be light, with a jacket or cardigan for evening. Most restaurants, except the most exclusive, do not require tie and jacket. Rome's pavements are often made of cobblestone, which are very harsh on the feet. Trainers or flat shoes are most suitable.

many exchange offices where you see the sign *cambio*, as the service is generally far simpler than that of a bank. They are also quicker and have longer opening hours, but they do take a rather large percentage for a transaction. Read the small print first. **Thomas Cook** (open daily) can be found at ✉ piazza Barberini 21, ☎ (06) 4202-0150, ✉ via del Corso 23, Stazione Colosseo or ✉ via della Conciliazione 23 (Vatican area), and **American Express** (open Mon–Sat) ✉ piazza di Spagna 38, ☎ (06) 67641, will exchange cheques and foreign currency.

By far the easiest way of obtaining currencies is from a *bancomat*, an automatic telling machine (ATM), using your credit or debit card and PIN number. All major banks offer this service – usually for a small fee. You will find ATMs in Piazza di Spagna, Termini, Via

Nazionale, Via Cavour, Vatican and Corso. **Lost (or stolen) credit cards** should be reported immediately to the respective issuing organization: AMEX, ☎ 8008 64046 or 800-874333 (toll free); Diner's Club, ☎ 800-864(06)4 (toll free); Mastercard, ☎ 800-870866 (toll free); Visa, ☎ 800-877232 (toll free).

Transport

Rome has an excellent and inexpensive public transport system. It is also easy to walk around. Bus maps are available from main metro stations and information offices. The best bargain for travel and sightseeing is the **Roma Pass**. **Tickets:** The same tickets are valid for all buses, trams and the metro within the city. The BIG ticket valid for one day costs €4, the three-day BIT ticket costs €11 and the weekly ticket is €16. A single ticket (€1) permits travel in one direction (with changes on all public transport systems to be completed within 75 minutes of validation). All tickets must be bought before boarding and are available from newspaper kiosks, metro stations, some bars and licensed *tabacchi*. They require validating on all transport.

Buses: Buses ply the city from 05:30 to midnight daily. Useful buses include the electric buses 116 and 117 near Via del Corso, which cover many ancient sites and modern shopping streets, and bus 64 from Piazza Cinquecento (opposite Stazione Termini) to the Vatican. Bus 590 follows the route taken by Metro Linea A (Vatican to Termini and out to Cinecittà) and offers facilities for handicapped passengers.

Metro: The metro, operated by **COTRAL**, is open 05:30–23:30 Sun–Fri, until 00:30

Sat. It has two arms which intersect at Stazione Termini. **Line A** runs eastwards from the Valle Aurelia via Cipro Musei Vaticani, the Spanish Steps, Termini and on towards San Giovanni in Laterano, Cinecittà and Anagnina. **Line B** runs from Rebibbia via Tiburtina to Termini, and then southwards, via the Colosseum, Pyramide and Ostiense to Laurentina.

Taxis: These are available from taxi ranks and can be flagged down in the street. Alternatively, taxis can be contacted by phone but incur a supplement for being called to your hotel or restaurant. To order a cab (in Italian, only), ☎ (06) 3570, (06) 6645, (06) 4994 or (06) 5551. Taxis are metered, but drivers tend to take you on an extended tour if they think you don't know your way around.

Two-wheels: The adventurous can **hire bikes** and **scooters** to

get around town. Contact **Bike e Scooter Rental**, via Cavour 80a, ☎ (06) 481 5669.

Business Hours

Food shops and markets start business around 07:30, closing for lunch around 12:30–13:00. Shops reopen in the afternoon around 16:00 until 19:00 or later. Fashion stores, which open Mon–Sat (and some on Sundays), rarely open before 10:30 and some close for lunch. Others remain open until 19:00 or 20:00. Banks open 08:30–13:30 and 14:45–15:45, Mon–Fri. Generally (although there are many variations), museums and monuments are open 09:00–19:00, Tue to Sat, and 09:00–13:00, Sun. Some private galleries operate different hours and close weekly on a day other than Mon.

Time

GMT + 1hr in winter; + 2hrs in summer.

Communications

Post: Mail can still be sluggish in Italy, with the exception of the new 24-hour delivery service (at a premium price). It is also slow outbound. Stamps for cards and letters can be bought from *tabacchi* (tobacconists), which are open longer hours than the post office. For packages and other mail, go to the Posta Centrale (Main Post Office), ⊠ piazza San Silvestro 19, ⊕ 08:30–20:00, Mon–Fri, and until noon on Sat, ☐ www.poste.it

Telephones: Mobile phones (*telefonini*) have made a huge impact in Italy, but there are still plenty of public phones operated by both coins or, more usually, a telephone card (*scheda telefonica*), available from news stands, post offices and *tabacchi*. Some telephone cabins accept international credit cards and others can even send faxes. Italy offers Home Direct dialling, and various toll-free numbers will link you with AT&T, MCI, Telstra, British Telecom and other international systems and debit your calls to your home account.

All numbers in Italy start with a '0' unless they are freephone numbers or for mobile telephones. You need to dial the '0' irrespective of where you are calling from in Italy, including calls within the same town. So, for dialling in Rome, you must dial '(06)' before the number. To dial out of the country, dial '00' followed by the country code and then the city or area code (without the '0' before it), and the number. For instance, a London number might be 00 44 20 7 624-8000. Dialling to Rome from overseas, keep the '(06)' code in the number.

Faxes: These may be sent from the post office, and also from a number of cabins around town.

Internet: Some of the most convenient include Museo del Corso, ⊠ via del Corso, 20 (Centre); Easy Everything, ⊠ via Barberini 2-16 (Centre); Bibli, ⊠ via del Fienaroli 28 (Trastevere); Caffé ⊠ Vicolo del Fico 17 (Navona); and the Internetcafé, ⊠ via dei Marrucini 12 (Termine).

Electricity

The current in Italy is 220V AC and plugs are two-pin, round ones.

Health Services

For medical help in English, contact Medline, via Parioli 166, ☎ (06) 808-0995 or the International Medical Centre, via Firenze 4, ☎ (06) 488-2371. Both are 24hr, private, multilingual services. English-speaking doctors can be found at Rome American Hospital, ⊠ via Emilio Longoni 69, ☎ (06) 22551. For pharmaceutical emergencies in English, visit ✉ piazza Barberini 49, ☎ (06) 482-5456 (24hr).

Personal Safety

Petty theft is Rome's main drawback. Bag-snatching and pick-pocketing are rife in tourist areas, Stazione Termini and on buses and trains during peak travel times. It is a good idea to carry cash and credit cards in a money belt. Keep belongings in sight (preferably in front of you), wear a camera or bag with a strap across the body, and be aware at all times. It is safe to travel alone in the evening on buses and the Metro but women should not do so at night. Carry a photo-copy of your passport in your wallet at all times and leave the passport, air tickets and other valuables in safe keeping at your hotel. If driving, do not leave anything inside the car.

Etiquette

It is polite to wear modest attire in a place of worship.

Language

Apart from the national language, **Italian**, many people also speak **English** and **French** (and **German** and **Spanish**). All efforts, however, to speak Italian are always appreciated. Grammar and pronun-ciation are both logi-cal, but there are a few things to remember. 'C' is hard (e.g. 'cat') unless followed by an 'I' or 'E', when it becomes 'Ch' (e.g. 'chair'). 'G' also remains hard (e.g. 'goat') unless softened by 'I' or 'E' (e.g. 'ger-bil'). 'CC' is the equiva-lent to the English 'CH' (e.g. 'church'). 'CH' at the beginning of a word is pro-nounced as a hard 'G' (e.g. 'guitar'). Use the polite *lei* (plu-ral) to strangers; you only use the second person singular, *tu*, for friends and children.

Useful Phrases

Good Day • *Buon Giorno*
Good Evening • *Buona Sera*
Hi or Bye • *Ciao*
Goodbye • *Arriverderci*
Please • *Per piacere*
Thanks • *Grazie*
Okay • *D'accordo*
Excuse me • *Mi scusi*
I'm sorry • *mi dispiace*
morning • *la mattina*
afternoon • *il pomeriggio*
night • *la notte*
How are you? • *Come sta?*
Fine, thanks • *Bene, grazie*
Help • *Aiuto*
I do not feel well • *Non mi sento bene*
Please call a doctor • *Chiami un medico per favore*
What time does it open • *A che ora apre?*
Where is? • *Dov'è?*
What time is it? • *Che ora è?*
Do you speak English? French? • *Parla Inglese? Francese?*
I don't understand • *Non capisco*
Please speak more slowly • *Parli più lentemente per favore*
Open • *aperto*
Closed • *chiuso*
How much does it cost, please? • *Per favore, quanto costa questo?* or *Quant' è per favore?*
Too expensive • *Troppo caro*
The bank • *la banca*
ATM • *il bancomat*
post office • *l'ufficio postale*
grocer's • *gli alimentari*
pharmacy • *la farmacia*

INDEX OF SIGHTS

GENERAL INDEX

GENERAL INDEX

General Index

General Index